Using Emerging Technologies to Develop Professional Learning

Internationally, there is a growing body of research about learners' responses to, and uses of, emerging technologies. However, the adoption of these technologies in teachers' professional development is still largely under-researched. Much of the existing literature still positions teachers as playing 'catch-up' in terms of using technology for teaching and learning in an ever expanding and changing world, and ignores the roles that these emerging technologies can play in teacher, and teacher educator, development and learning.

This book aims to address the lack of research in the area, and it contributes to the new knowledge area of how emerging technologies can effectively address professional learning, drawing on case studies and perspectives from across the world. Contributors use a wide variety of approaches to analyse the potential for emerging (and established) technologies, including digital, Web2.0, social media, and IT tools, to develop 'effective' or 'deep' professional learning for pre- and in-service teachers and teacher educators.

This book was originally published as a special issue of *Professional Development in Education*.

Jean Murray is Professor of Education in the Cass School at the University of East London, UK. Her research focuses on the sociological analysis of teacher education policies and practices in the UK and internationally. She has a particular interest in the identities and career trajectories of teacher educators. Jean has written many books, articles and other publications, and participated in numerous national and international research projects. She has been an active member of the academic community in the UK and internationally for many years.

Warren Kidd is Senior Lecturer and a teacher educator at the Cass School of Education and Communities at the University of East London, UK, where he supports the professional development and professional learning of teachers, trainee teachers, and staff across a wide variety of educational sectors. He is the Programme Leader for Humanities Secondary Initial Teacher Education and for the Masters in Learning and Teaching in Higher Education. His scholarly interests explore teacher identity, how to support new teachers with practice, and the use of digital and mobile learning both inside and outside the classroom.

Using Emerging Technologies to Develop Professional Learning

Edited by
Jean Murray and Warren Kidd

Routledge
Taylor & Francis Group

LONDON AND NEW YORK

First published 2016
by Routledge
2 Park Square, Milton Park, Abingdon, Oxon, OX14 4RN, UK

and by Routledge
711 Third Avenue, New York, NY 10017, USA

Routledge is an imprint of the Taylor & Francis Group, an informa business

British Library Cataloguing in Publication Data
A catalogue record for this book is available from the British Library

ISBN 13: 978-1-138-18644-6

Typeset in Times
by RefineCatch Limited, Bungay, Suffolk

Publisher's Note
The publisher accepts responsibility for any inconsistencies that may have
arisen during the conversion of this book from journal articles to book chapters,
namely the possible inclusion of journal terminology.

Disclaimer
Every effort has been made to contact copyright holders for their permission to
reprint material in this book. The publishers would be grateful to hear from any
copyright holder who is not here acknowledged and will undertake to rectify
any errors or omissions in future editions of this book.

Contents

Citation Information

The chapters in this book were originally published in *Professional Development in Education*, volume 39, issue 2 (April 2013). When citing this material, please use the original page numbering for each article, as follows:

Editorial

Using emerging technologies to develop professional learning
Warren Kidd and Jean Murray
Professional Development in Education, volume 39, issue 2 (April 2013) pp. 165–167

Chapter 1

Second look – second think: a fresh look at video to support dialogic feedback in peer coaching
Jennifer Charteris and Dianne Smardon
Professional Development in Education, volume 39, issue 2 (April 2013) pp. 168–185

Chapter 2

The 'trainer in your pocket': mobile phones within a teacher continuing professional development program in Bangladesh
Christopher S. Walsh, Tom Power, Masuda Khatoon, Sudeb Kumar Biswas, Ashok Kumar Paul, Bikash Chandra Sarkar and Malcolm Griffiths
Professional Development in Education, volume 39, issue 2 (April 2013) pp. 186–200

Chapter 3

Professional learning to support elementary teachers' use of the iPod Touch in the classroom
Katia Ciampa and Tiffany L. Gallagher
Professional Development in Education, volume 39, issue 2 (April 2013) pp. 201–221

Chapter 4

Research capacity-building with new technologies within new communities of practice: reflections on the first year of the Teacher Education Research Network
Zoe Fowler, Grant Stanley, Jean Murray, Marion Jones and Olwen McNamara
Professional Development in Education, volume 39, issue 2 (April 2013) pp. 222–239

For any permission-related enquiries please visit:
http://www.tandfonline.com/page/help/permissions

INTRODUCTION

Using emerging technologies to develop professional learning

This special issue locates teachers' professional learning within an 'emerging' or 'new' technologies framework. We define such technologies as including digital, Web2.0, social media, mobile and information technology tools. In compiling the issue, we recognised that, whilst some research on the adoption of such tools and technologies in teachers' professional development has been produced, this is still an emerging area of practice. Also, the forms and effectiveness of such provision in promoting teacher learning at various career 'stages' are decidedly under-researched areas. The value placed upon technologies by teachers and teacher educators and their potential in professional learning are therefore often ambiguous and in need of a (re)new(ed) focus of attention.

Internationally, there is a growing body of research (and speculation) about adult learners' responses to and uses of emerging technologies. But much of the literature on teachers' professional development still conceptualises teachers as playing 'catch-up' with the world outside schools in terms of their use of technology. Consequently, some professional development courses essentially focus on developing and auditing the technological competence and skills of teachers. Other types of professional development provision prioritise the adoption of e-learning pedagogies or the deployment of specific types of new technologies in schools, often in superficial ways. Ironically, these types of provision often ignore the roles these very same technologies can play as the conduits for teacher – and teacher educator – development and learning.

This special issue aims to contribute to developing knowledge about the roles that new technologies can play in the creation and implementation of good-quality professional development programmes. It draws on papers from both national and international perspectives, bringing together papers from Bangladesh, Canada, New Zealand and the USA, as well as the United Kingdom. The issue explores issues for professional learning through and with technologies, whilst centring on issues of professional development, rather than just on the technology itself. Its unique contribution to the field of teacher education lies in analysing ways in which emerging (and established) technologies may – or may not – have the potential to facilitate 'effective' or 'deep' professional learning for pre-service and in-service teachers.

We focus first on the benefits of specific technologies and tools, considering how they might aid teacher learning and enable professional development, often across time–space boundaries. The contributions cross in-service and pre-service distinctions and include a focus on teachers from all sectors of the school system and on into the lifelong learning and higher education sectors. Questions we would wish to pose here include: Can emergent and older technologies facilitate 'deep' and long-lasting professional learning? Are technologies positioned to allow for in-depth reflection by practitioners? To what extent do teachers feel that they 'own' professional development mediated through technology? How might the use of new technologies bridge time, space and distance to support continuing professional development for diverse groups of teachers? And how are the perceived benefits of technology for teachers' learning perceived by organisations, educational leaders and teacher educators and, of course, by teachers themselves?

We start this issue with a contribution by Jennifer Charteris and Dianne Smardon in New Zealand, which evaluates the outcomes of a case study using video to develop professional learning. Video technology is not a new tool, of course, but it has often been used in superficial ways in the past. This research employs a fresh way of using video to develop 'deep learning' during peer coaching sessions. Here the study findings indicated that teacher participants were able to 'see' themselves thinking, in the process becoming explicitly aware of their peer coaching role and personal learning processes. This opportunity, to have a 'second look, second think', allowed the teachers to think further and more deeply on the learning dialogue, affording additional insights to their practices.

Examples of mobile phones being used with teachers to provide continuing professional development, particularly in emerging economies and at scale, are largely absent in the research literature. But our second paper by Christopher Walsh and his co-authors explores a large-scale programme in Bangladesh using mobile phones. Here those phones are part of English in Action's model for providing teachers across this vast and under-developed country with professional development to improve their communicative language teaching. The paper describes how, in the current part of the programme, low-cost mobile phones are used as 'the trainer in the pocket' for numerous teachers in remote locations. Based on their findings, the authors argue that such use of mobile phones for the provision of teacher development at scale is highly effective, timely and replicable in both developed and developing contexts.

The next paper by Katia Ciampa and Tiffany Gallagher considers how teachers in an elementary school (ages 5–13) in Canada learn about mobile multi-media devices in order to extend and enhance their classroom practice. In this example we see how teachers are supported to learn about the iPod Touch as a classroom tool and to gain confidence to integrate the technology into their pedagogy. Interestingly, here the iPod Touch is the designated learning medium for both teachers and children. This paper proposes a framework that outlines particular characteristics for supporting teachers' effective integration of mobile multimedia technology into classroom practice. It also raises the important issues of leadership and management, particularly in the creation of strong e-cultures for teaching within a school.

The fourth paper is written by Grant Stanley, Zoe Fowler and the founders of the Teacher Education Research Network (TERN), a large-scale capacity-building programme funded by the Economic and Social Research Council in England to strengthen research in and on teacher education. As the authors note, there is significant interest in how new technologies support learning across higher education. In this case, the TERN project used virtual research environments, with somewhat mixed results, to facilitate communication, networking and learning by the researchers, all of whom were teacher educators. Using the theoretical lenses of situated learning and socio-cultural approaches to literacy, the paper analyses the participants' ways of engaging with this technology. In conclusion, the authors outline a range of factors that they believe are important for successful engagement with new technologies in future academic communities of practice.

This is followed by a paper from Nancy Fichtman Dana and her co-authors, which explores a case study in the USA focusing on professional development for teachers working in virtual schools. Virtual school teachers teach completely online courses and do not reside or work within proximate geographical locations or time zones in the USA. The professional development programme for such teachers that this case study designed was therefore supported by the use of various synchronous and asynchronous technology tools during a year-long collaborative action research endeavour. This paper provides insights into what constitutes powerful professional learning for this unusual group of teachers, as well as looking at the ways in which synchronous and asynchronous technology tools can be utilised to scaffold that learning. The questions posed here include: What does the use of these new technologies add to the action research design of the programme and what additional benefits did the teachers gain from learning in a virtual world?

In the next paper Warren Kidd considers the use of Web2.0 tools and platforms in the education of beginning teachers on pre-service programmes in England. He argues that the use of technological tools during pre-service supports the development of teacher competence and reflective practice, alongside generating essential learning about e-learning practices. Through both learning to teach and – eventually – teaching their own pupils using new technologies, e-learning pedagogies come to form an essential part of the 'craft repertoires' of these new teachers. This is particularly important since these teachers are starting their careers in the rapidly expanding technological environments of twenty-first-century schools and colleges. Kidd also suggests that technology might offer a counter-point to prevalent performativity cultures and neo-liberal discourse in debates about pre-service teachers' professional learning in England.

Taken together, the examples of teacher learning in this issue present different technologies as effective tools to enable synchronous and asynchronous 'deep' professional learning over distances and for sustained periods of time. Like many conventional forms of professional development, the programmes described here all privilege the importance of communication, interaction and dialogue for teachers' professional learning, but offer new and sometimes more effective ways of achieving those key touchstones through the use of technology.

The final paper considers possible ways forward in terms of using new technologies to enhance and strengthen teachers' professional knowledge bases. The paper by Marilyn Leask and Sarah Younie, drawing on their work over many years and in many varying contexts, poses the starting question of why so little attention is drawn to the knowledge bases available to support teachers in improving the quality of their professional knowledge. The paper argues that the quality of these knowledge bases and teacher access to them is often taken for granted in research on professional learning and is rarely acknowledged in the discourses of school improvement. It then goes on to examine the unacknowledged problem of providing a sustained approach to improving the quality of and access to the evidence bases underpinning professional development programmes. Finally, the authors outline opportunities that exist for low-cost, interlinked national and international e-infrastructures to be developed to support their ideals of knowledge sharing and building across teaching communities.

Warren Kidd and Jean Murray
University of East London, London, UK

Second look – second think: a fresh look at video to support dialogic feedback in peer coaching

Jennifer Charteris and Dianne Smardon

Faculty of Education, The University of Waikato, Hamilton, New Zealand

This case study, concerning peer coaching for sustainable professional practice, utilised video to enable teachers 'deep learning' during peer coaching sessions. While the use of video is not a new tool for continuing professional development, this research employs a fresh way of using it. Teachers reflected on their learning process by watching video footage filmed during group peer coaching sessions. The study explores how this reflection with peers influenced the teachers' thinking and decision-making. Findings indicated that teacher participants were able to 'see' themselves thinking, becoming more explicitly aware of their peer coaching role and their own professional learning processes. This paper links strongly to the theme of this special issue, advancing that the use of video can enable teachers a unique opportunity to review and reflect on their positioning in their professional learning. The research recommends ongoing exploration of practices that afford teachers opportunities to develop metacognitive awareness and an agentic role in their own learning.

Introduction

In this paper we argue that digital tools can afford teachers new ways to promote deep learning during peer coaching situations. It is our contention that teachers can go beyond superficial learning in collaboration with their colleagues to grow sustainable practices though the use of information technologies. In this research paper we address how a collaborative community of inquiry can be enhanced through the use of video as a tool for reflection. In the New Zealand teacher professional learning context, video has been utilised predominantly to examine teacher classroom practice. The teacher participants in this study use video to reflect on their learning from previous collaborative peer coaching sessions. This opportunity, to have a 'second look, second think', allowed teacher participants to think further and more deeply on their learning dialogue, affording additional insights. This is a fresh approach to the use of video. While classroom video footage has been used for stimulus recall in teacher peer coaching (van Es 2010, Cutrim Schmid 2011, Stover *et al.* 2011), the specific use of video in the development of teacher peer coaching skills is less prevalent. In this study, video is an integral tool that enables teacher participants to reflect on the process of peer coaching, their roles in it and, at the same time, have a further chance to engage with their professional learning inquiry. Through viewing peer coaching video footage, teachers became more aware of their own professional learning processes. This opportunity to have a second look supported the teachers to think further and more deeply on their learning dialogue, affording further insights and realisations. The use of video supported and strengthened the teachers' communities of inquiry.

Situated in a New Zealand context, the writers from The University of Waikato Assess to Learn team have been involved in providing 'assessment for learning' continuing professional development (CPD) for teachers over the last nine years. Here, students are positioned at the heart of the assessment process where they actively collaborate with their teachers to develop their capability to assess their own learning (Absolum *et al.* 2009). While many definitions of assessment for learning prevail, we draw upon a short, second-generation definition where:

> Assessment for Learning is part of everyday practice by students, teachers and peers that seeks, reflects upon and responds to information from dialogue, demonstration and observation in ways that enhance ongoing learning. (Klenowski 2009, p. 264)

In our work with teachers we have observed that the use of a dialogic process to interpret and make sense of student voice and teacher talk data has potential to enhance teacher engagement, stimulate a careful and thorough analysis of the data and support practitioners to identify next steps in their professional learning. As CPD providers we assist teachers and school leaders to develop cohesive school-wide assessment practices and processes, give effect to the New Zealand Curriculum and develop their expertise with 'Teaching as Inquiry' (Ministry of Education 2007, p. 35). These practices and processes include a peer coaching model that we facilitated as in-service teacher educators.

We are concerned with teachers' perceptions of what deliberate actions support their professional learning processes. Teachers are often positioned as the passive consumers of research that will assist them to make decisions. As educators strive to 'get it right' in a performative culture, they are marketed research that defines quality and shapes their practice. Embedded in a technical rational approach to schooling improvement and reform is the mantra 'what works will work'. However, research can only show us what has been possible; it can only tell us what has worked but cannot tell us 'what works' generically (Biesta 2007, p. 8). According to Wiliam:

> ... researchers have underestimated the complexity of what it is that teachers do, and in particular, have failed to understand how great an impact context has on teachers' practice. That is why 'what works?' is not the right question, because everything works somewhere, and nothing works everywhere. (2006, p. 8)

In this paper we share the findings of our research into how reflections with peers influenced teachers' thinking and decision-making. While these findings relate specifically to this research situation, it is our hope that our readers can make connections to other contexts. We observed that through the use of video teachers became explicitly aware of peer coaching as a dialogic process that enhanced their professional learning. The teachers engaged in metacognitive reflection, 'seeing' themselves thinking and noticing their decision-making processes. They recognised when they determined their next-step actions for their teaching. Through viewing videoed peer coaching footage the teachers were able to transform what had previously been subjective into an object for examination. Furthermore, the video allowed the teacher participants to have a 'second look' and 'second think'. The video as a mediated tool afforded the teachers additional insights into their previous dialogue and thinking. They were able to think further about both peer coaching as a learning process and their actions for their own classroom practice.

The research suggests that there is value in the use of video to support a dialogic feedback process, where teachers are agentic co-learners and co-constructers of knowledge. This contrasts with a position in which teachers are 'absorbers' or passive recipients of knowledge constructed elsewhere, which has been described as a transmission process or training model of CPD (Kennedy 2005, p. 237). We acknowledge that there is an inherent complexity in teachers identifying and recognising what is at the forefront of their colleagues' thinking and this research positions itself within a transformative model of CPD. This is a teacher-centred, context-specific model of CPD with a focus on communities of inquiry, a step beyond the traditional communities of practice notion. It draws from coaching and mentoring, communities of practice and action research models for the CPD as a transformative approach to professional learning (Kennedy 2005). The transformative model is at the opposite end of a continuum to the transmission model of CPD with its focus on teachers as agentic inquirers.

When we think about the notion of active learners we consider Mezirow's (1997) theory of transformational learning, which as a process of exploring assumptions enables practitioners to become more reflective and critical, being more open to the ideas of others and accepting of ideas, which is the foundation of deep learning as conceptualised in this study.

Dialogic peer coaching

According to Robbins (1991), collaborative peer coaching is a confidential process in which two or more professional colleagues work together to reflect on current practices, expanding, refining and building new skills, sharing ideas, teaching one another, conducting classroom research or solving problems in the workplace. Peer coaching has nothing to do with evaluation. It is not intended as a remedial activity or strategy to 'fix' teachers (Robbins 1991). Rather than giving 'how to' advice, we view this 'sharing' as a peer coach to be more like active listening, a stance that enables peers to struggle to make sense of their own practice. McArdle and Coutts (2010) critique individualistic notions of reflective practice, advocating for the added dimensions of shared sense-making and collaborative engagement for professional renewal. This idea of shared sense-making for action and change is a self-monitoring and self-monitored social process that extends the concept of reflective practice.

Dialogic peer coaching relationships can support teachers' reflective dialogue where they co-construct new ideas, ways of thinking and new learning. In these dialogic relationships it is possible to see things from at least two perspectives at once (Wegerif 2008), one's own and a peer coach's. Teachers can take time to explore and ponder ideas with their peers as a resource (Carnell and Lodge 2002). Nehring *et al.* (2010, p. 400) define reflective dialogue as, 'reflection with others characterised by careful listening, active questioning and an openness to potentially profound change to one's beliefs'. Active listening is central to reflective dialogue. Freed (2003) describes four behaviours integral to reflective dialogue. These comprise suspending judgment, voicing issues, listening actively and respecting others. An active listening process is one that enables participants to risk take in disclosing their own views:

> Listening means allowing what the other says to break through one's own preconceptions and prejudgments. And speaking involves risking one's own ideas by offering them to the group as a potential way to interpret truth or right action. Quality conversation is a dialogue in which each participant risks changing one's mind or attitudes in the process of working towards mutual understanding. (Deakin Crick and Joldersma 2007, p. 92)

Through dialogue, teachers can reflect on their own experiences through the lens of others and, in doing so, engage in cumulative talk. Borrowing from Alexander's (2005) classroom-based notion of cumulative talk, we use this term to describe how teachers' thinking connects with the thinking and ideas of their peers.

The most promising forms of professional development engage teachers in the collaborative investigation of genuine problems over time, in ways that significantly affect their practice (Lom and Sullenger 2011). According to Wiliam (2008), teacher learning communities appear to be the most effective, practical method of changing day-to-day classroom practices. A process of collaborative inquiry can enable practitioners to critically reflect on the evidence they gather, enhancing their own and their students' learning. A key feature of this collaborative inquiry is the use of video to stimulate this reflection. The peer coaching approach outlined in this paper is embedded in the socio-cultural environments of classrooms, schools and communities.

A critical aspect of reflection can be integral to teachers' learning. We draw from Brookfield (1995), who suggests that by utilising different lenses on our thinking we can critique our assumptions. Collaborative critical reflection enables a dialogic community of peers, who share a commitment, to explore their assumptions. This process is based on personal experiences. It involves imagining and exploring alternatives to current assumptions. Those who reflect critically are self-aware and often become more sceptical of the world around them (Franz 2007). Wagenheim *et al.* describe the impact of transformational inquiry for teachers:

> Through a regular cycle of reflective inquiry – surfacing and challenging assumptions – teachers seeking improvement seek transformative change; change in their 'way of being' as a teacher, not just in their 'way of doing.' Becoming a better teacher is about reflecting on and questioning deeply held assumptions in an experiential cycle of inquiry, developing new strategies, testing in action, and learning. It is through reflection and resultant self-knowledge that one can leverage greater awareness of others and course content in the journey toward becoming a better teacher. (2009, p. 504)

Video is a tool that can support peer coaches to grow in their role. Peer coaches need to know when and how to pose questions (Robertson 2005) that may assist reflection. Through viewing videoed footage, peer coaches can observe how they question to promote thinking and engage in active listening. This process of active listening and questioning is a form of dialogic feedback that contrasts with the frequently adopted collegial role of 'advice dispenser' and 'solution provider'.

Feedback as advice serves as an external evaluation and can be described as a 'gift' that may be neither wanted nor acted upon. This often uninvited form of feedback may not necessarily be the learner's focus. Watkins (2000) suggests that at times the responsibility of the two parties in the feedback process can become distorted, with the peer giving feedback taking responsibility for the other person's development, setting targets for the other person to achieve while the recipient is positioned passively. The use of video can enable teachers to construct their own feedback utilising primary data rather than receiving feedback through the lens of another. In this way the traditional power relationship of giver and receiver of feedback is destabilised.

In contrast, Game and Metcalfe (2009) view every response and every recognition in a dialogue as feedback. This form of symbiotic feedback where learners engage in reciprocal peer coaching is meaningful because it is a simultaneous process where people are learning from each other. Askew and Lodge (2000, p. 13) take a 'co-constructivist' view of feedback, describing how it can be constructed through loops of dialogue and information exchanged between peers. Orland-Barak (2006) highlights that any one utterance may encompass not only the 'voice' of the person talking, but also the voice of the person the utterance is directed to, the voice of the addressee, as well as other voices gained from previous life experiences, from our history and our culture. The presence of another person can surface ideas as the speaker considers the perspectives of their audience.

By capturing the peer coaching dialogue on video, the co-constructed meanings of utterances have the potential for greater visibility for those participating in the process. Teachers can be open to new possibilities within the liminal. Somerville (2007) describes the liminal as a space of becoming in between one state of being and another, where one is working at the limit or the edge of self. Ravenscroft *et al.* (2007) consider that the boundary between participants in a dialogue is not a demarcation line, or an external link between self and other, but an inclusive 'space' within which self and other mutually construct and reconstruct each other. This can be described as a liminal space that can afford what is unseen to become seen.

In order to think about a concept and shift it from being 'taken for granted' to the forefront of thinking, there is a need for reflective practitioners to re-view and re-position. Kegan and Laskow (2009) assert that if we want to increase mental complexity, we need to move aspects of our meaning-making from subject to object. Hence our way of knowing or making meaning becomes a kind of 'tool' that we possess and can control or use, rather than something that controls us. What is subject is invisible. This is what we look through, the way we view the world. When we move from subject to object, what was once an unconscious lens now becomes something that can be seen and reflected upon (Garvey Berger 2006). Citing Kegan (1994), Garvey Berger writes that:

> 'We have object; we are subject' (p. 32). Things that are Object in our lives are 'those elements of our knowing or organizing that we can reflect on, handle, look at, be responsible for, relate to each other, take control of, internalize, assimilate, or otherwise operate upon (1994, p. 32)'. (Garvey Berger 2002, p. 36)

This change of focus allows teachers to see with fresh eyes.

In teacher CPD, video is most commonly used to record classroom episodes for stimulus recall purposes. This study positions video as a feedback tool that assists teachers to look at their process of professional learning through peer coaching and a second chance for reflection on their teacher inquiry. The literature suggests that collaborative peer coaching with a specific focus on reflective dialogue can assist teachers to inquire into their practice and is a form of professional learning based in authentic, contextually relevant situations. Through dialogic feedback, teachers can be afforded an agentic role in their learning. By developing peer coaching processes of reflective dialogue in communities of practice, teachers can invest in their peer relationships and become resources for each other as they engage with their real-world issues. Drawing from Kegan's notion of making subject object, our view is that liminal spaces between interlocutors are important places to explore if deep teacher learning is to take place. Through video we were able to capture the workings of these intermediary spaces.

Research method

This case-study research explicitly focuses on how teachers can collaboratively use a dialogic approach to peer coaching, to mine and interpret their classroom observation data through the use of video. The research examines facilitated inquiry where groups of two or three teachers engaged in a formal process of collaborative dialogue over two years. Although the study is set in an assessment for learning CPD context, we would argue that the processes are readily transferable. Using video as a mediated tool, this study explores two main questions:

(1) What happens when teachers focus on and interpret their assessment classroom observation data collaboratively?
(2) How can teachers reflect on their part in this process in order to identify the factors that contribute to clarity for their next learning steps?

There were 13 teacher peer coach participants from five schools, a convenient sample in that the participants were those that responded to an invitation to participate in the research. We appreciate that this is not a sample that can be used to generalise based on the participants' experiences, but the use of video is relatable to the readers of this research. Bassey judges relateability to be:

> ... an important criterion for judging the merit of a case study. Relateability is the extent to which the details are sufficient and appropriate for a teacher working in a similar situation to relate his [or her] decision making to that described in the case study. (Bassey 1981 cited in Bell 2006, p. 11)

Participants were aware of the difference between the CPD project and the research and were able to withdraw at any time. The researchers were primarily participant observers as they operated within the communities of practice. The researchers acknowledge their positioning and the power structures that will always be present as they are external agents within the context of schools.

Participants used the video data reflexively to reflect on their own practice and processes as researchers. Student and teacher voice data were collected during classroom observations. These data collection tools were used because they were unobtrusive and contextually located. The teachers then analysed and critically explored their data through a peer coaching process of collaborative dialogue. The dialogue protocols for this peer coaching process were established with the teacher participants at the outset of the research project. The following characteristics were adopted to define dialogue:

- suspension of judgment;
- release of our need for a specific outcome;
- an inquiry into an examination of underlying assumptions;
- authenticity;
- a slower pace of interaction with silence between speakers;
- listening deeply to self and others for collective meaning. (Ellinor and Gerard 1998 in Sparks 2005, p. 2)

Through peer coaching dialogue the teachers developed questions based on their classroom practice and determined their next-step actions to support student learning. The groups met formally for peer coaching once a term. These peer coach meetings were videoed. The video footage was burned as an individual DVD copy for each teacher, which they then viewed in their own time with reference to the following three questions:

(1) At which point did you determine your next-step action in the DVD?
(2) What do you think led you to make your decision at this point?
(3) How did reflecting with others influence your thinking and decision-making?

Each teacher was interviewed in the fortnight following their guided self-review of the DVD at a mutually determined time. The intention of these interviews was to learn more about the teachers' perspectives on the process of peer coaching. These individual teacher interviews were video-recorded and transcribed. Using a constant-comparison method of analysis (Cohen *et al.* 2007), the researchers separately reviewed the transcripts of the teacher interviews from the videos, then collaboratively noted codes; clarifying, rationalising and fine-tuning them through dialogue. Through this process of inductive analysis, patterns, themes and categories emerged from the data rather than being determined prior to our data collection and analysis (Patton 1990). To triangulate these data we supplemented the interviews with an online questionnaire. The questionnaire responses verified the themes that had been established. These were then member-checked with the teachers (Lincoln and Guba 1985).

The following themes were generated from the data: video enhanced dialogic peer coaching, making the subject object and the opportunity to have a 'second look' and 'second think' through reviewing video footage. These themes are supported and illustrated by a sample from the teacher voice data. The data suggest that the use of video can assist teachers both to think deeply and to strengthen a collaborative community of inquiry.

Video enhancement of dialogic peer coaching

The use of video provides a tool for teacher reflection. By closely viewing the footage, teachers reflect on their professional learning processes and identify roles within the peer coaching relationships. The teachers observe pivotal moments in their thinking that were previously hidden and now become visible to them when they watch the DVD. The teachers note that through the peer coaching dialogues they clarify their own thinking. As they listen to the stories of others, they relate them to their own lives. In turn, when teachers tell their own stories they are cognisant of how their colleagues make meaning from their story. The presence of the video recorder can influence teachers to focus their thinking.

Aware that the conversation is recorded, Dee wants to remain focused on the purpose of the professional peer coaching session. Dee observes how the presence of the video supports her reflection:

> Maybe the video makes you more responsible for what you are saying. It keeps you on track. You don't want to be waffling around … [You are] a little more serious and focused. (Dee)

Trudy sees that the professional dialogue, captured on the DVD, inspires and motivates her. She notes that the peer coaching dialogue builds back and forth cumulatively:

> What I get so much out of it is the motivation and the inspiration from my colleagues. You know, it's ACTION! What I love most about it is that it's really thoughtful, focused conversation about something specific. And there's her ideas and then mine and back and forth and I do find it really motivating and inspiring and I think that's the biggest thing for me. (Trudy)

Having seen her DVD footage, Belinda employs digging as a metaphor to illustrate the depth of her thinking visible to her on the DVD:

> You are talking you have to think and dig really deep down into your own thinking. That's something that whole process of having to articulate, you have to dig into your thinking. (Belinda)

Belinda also notes that she makes new connections through her cumulative talk with colleagues on the DVD. She thinks through the process further and makes a judgement about how one can remain 'narrow minded' when thinking alone. In addition, she acknowledges how the presence of her peer coach aids her to go to a deeper level in her thinking, more so than if she had been reflecting alone:

> Do it by yourself? You don't really. You're so narrow-minded in your thinking. Because the whole thing is happening with just yourself and you are comparing and thinking about things which are happening in your own practice. You don't often tend to ever go outside that. The minute that somebody else is in the conversation you are having to clarify things in more detail. You are bouncing off some idea that they may have. It doesn't even matter if the people know your students or not because then you go into even deeper levels. Because you are having to explain it to somebody else, it's much deeper. With yourself it's very surface. (Belinda)

Like Belinda, on viewing the DVD Louisa recognises that the dialogic process scaffolds her thinking more than reflecting alone:

> I might be sitting looking at my own data. I come to a point [and] I think 'Oh I might try this.' But sometimes just that sharing of someone else's experience helps you go 'Oh yeah!' Or it might be building on something you might have thought [about] or you might be thinking about. But it just helps you scaffold that. (Louisa)

Louisa recognises that her moments of insight and realisation happen with her peer coaches through the dialogic process that she views in the footage:

> Through talking with others I might have a couple of 'hows' going on in my brain or sometimes I might even go 'how can I fix that' and not actually have an idea. But it's through talking with others that the light bulb [goes on]. (Louisa)

Jane sees on the DVD how her colleagues' stories are a catalyst to her own thinking. She acknowledges that their ideas are helpful as they talk through the innovations that they are trialling in their practice:

> Not so much what they would do if they were in my shoes. With them talking about what they might be doing with their children … I think – that might work for me. (Jane)

Louisa's own body language provides visual cues that give her an insight into her process of learning when she watches the DVD. She witnesses her thinking process:

> As I was talking I could see myself 'cos I know my own body language and even facial expressions. I knew I was thinking – I'm thinking on the spot now, you know what mean and so I could see myself doing it … It was good because the more I talked the more you could see me processing it as I went and then I would come to a conclusion. (Louisa)

Through watching herself think, Louisa also notices that her thinking takes time. She can see on the video where the pieces fall into place for her and she generates a new way of thinking about her practice:

> It's the talking about it that helps me go blip, blip, blip around in a circle 'cause I listen to myself and I was thinking 'Oh god when am I actually going to get to it?' I must admit when I was watching it I was thinking 'When am I going …' As I was watching the video I was going 'Well yeah' 'cause some things seem so obvious why am I not coming out with it straight away but I had to do a whole lot of talking before I got to that. (Louisa)

Dee can see that she experiences a form of dissonance. The dialogue results in 'an uneasy feeling' for her that prompts further reflection. Although the process can be disconcerting, Dee acknowledges the role of questioning in the peer coach relationship. The presence of peer coaches can act as a catalyst to enable teachers to problematise the taken for granted, making the familiar strange. There is a collaborative focus to improve. Dee explains how she reasons, troubling normality and the taken for granted:

> Sometimes you do need to just go, 'Hmm, why are we doing this again?' Somebody else has to do it to you. Because it's actually not very comfortable to have to justify inside your head, why are we doing this? And could we do it better? If someone's given you that uneasy feeling, it keeps popping back into your head when you do get that feeling you can't leave it. You have to then come back and have that conversation again. (Dee)

The DVD enables Kevin to reflect on the process of his thinking. Through seeing himself talking he recognises how he positions himself theoretically:

> While I was talking on the video – it didn't come out in the video but I was subconsciously realising where I was placing myself at that time – you know where I was within my overall class. (Kevin)

Louisa observes from the DVD how her thinking is not a linear, direct process and can be slow and time consuming:

> … what I noticed about myself is I talk round and round and round in cycles and then I go aaarh! (Louisa)

The viewing of peer coaching video footage assisted the teachers to notice and recognise their peer coaching and professional learning processes. They had insights and realisations through this viewing.

Making the subject object – seeing oneself seen

When viewing the peer coaching footage the teachers 'see' themselves thinking. This surfaces notions and ideas that have previously been subjective, making them an object they can see from another angle. This metacognitive reflection enables teachers to notice their thinking and decision-making processes. Thus, they are able to recognise when they determine their next steps. Through the use of the video, teachers objectify their thinking.

Andy sees himself in action. The tool enables him to recognise that he is confident in his own voice. It presents an opportunity for him to self-reflect and feedback to himself – through this interview:

> It was really interesting to watch myself, I guess, 'cause like everybody's kind of self-conscious. But to watch it, I did a really good job, even though I wasn't consciously trying to. I did a good job of listening. And my body language was really neat. Whereas [usually] I think I slouch not listening to the person [but] I'm alright. When it was my turn to speak I spoke well I felt – and I knew what I wanted to say. (Andy)

Belinda speaks of the need to clarify her ideas so that her peer coach builds an understanding of what is important to her. Talking with another person surfaces the evidence 'in the back of her head', enabling her to shift what is subjective in her thinking to objectify it:

> [By] sitting down and talking to somebody else, you really have to clarify your thinking so while the evidence was sitting in the back of my head I wasn't really clear. (Belinda)

The video is a record of Belinda's learning and an opportunity to notice the detail of what is going on for her. She comments on her physical responses as she challenges her own thinking:

The body language. I could see where it was getting difficult. I was having to really think. How watching it and having to notice in a lot more detail, what was going on, and of course it's a record of your next steps and where you're going with it. It's more meaningful and it gives a deeper picture. (Belinda)

Louisa also watches herself thinking as she makes sense of the collegial dialogue. She considers the possibilities of her peer's initiative for her own classroom context:

I could even see myself [think] in the video – only because I know me, I guess. I was watching my eyes and I could see my brain ticking over 'Oh yeah that's a good idea!' and then 'Ooh how can I make that work in my classroom?' And I could see that happening. (Louisa)

Through viewing the DVD Belinda is surprised to note how her actual process of thinking is slow. When she looks at herself objectively she can 'see' her reflection process taking place through the dialogue:

It's quite interesting actually watching through the video. Because at the start I knew exactly when I decided [on my next steps]. But when you watch the video and I'm watching myself and seeing the thinking there. You can almost see the thought process happening because you know what's happening or you think you do. (Belinda)

During the reflective dialogue meeting, Kay was 'in the moment'. The process of making the subject object through watching the DVD was a catalyst for Kay to further her thinking and determine the action she was going to take:

I actually found watching the DVD really enlightening. I found that when we were in here in the room you're going over [it in your head] thinking about what happened and people are firing questions at you. I actually found watching the DVD more where I got to my next step than actually when we were in here. (Kay)

Through the peer coaching dialogue, Kay was 'sticking' to her plan while her peers asked her questions to encourage her to engage in critical reflection. However, when she objectifies her positioning in the dialogue she can see her colleagues' role in challenging her thinking. The video affords her an opportunity to think dialogically:

I think that when I was in here that time I was sticking to my plan but then I could see that happening on the video and I was 'oh hang on a minute, they're quite right on asking these questions 'cause that's something I do need to think about.' (Kay)

Andy looks in from out, objectifying himself as the subject. The use of the video affords him the distance to be objective:

[When I watched the DVD it was] not just through what I was saying. My body language and the way I listened 'cause obviously you have a funny idea of yourself looking out from your eyes – you don't normally see in. (Andy)

In this second interview Belinda theorises her process of seeing herself thinking. There were three things happening: reviewing data, processing data and talking about the data. Belinda's thinking becomes visible to her. She sees the direction of her thinking as a visual reminder:

> Looking at the student voice and then, thinking about it and being asked, having to explain to somebody else. It's all happening at the same time. What caused it was having to talk about it. I think, I would hate to see what is going on inside my head, because you're speaking, but in the head there's lots of other things happening and we have to talk about it. Stop, think and I think I did a stop, think and you can see me on the video. That's when – then having to speak it, articulate what I thought. (Belinda)

Belinda connects with her peer coaches' comments through having a fresh look at the coaching session:

> … but it was watching the video of our dialogue about that. That was really powerful 'cause you can't, well I can't, remember everything that I've said. Watching the video I could see the point where I was thinking that, and where the train of thought was going and where the conversation was going. You could see why it went that way. (Belinda)

Clive describes how reviewing the DVD enables him to take a bird's eye view and shift what is subject or invisible in his thinking to object and obvious to him:

> … um I heard her say it that day but it didn't give me a jolt me then … but having the time to look at the video later, the film later – it was a different context 'cos it's more intense. I guess your brain's in a different place. You are listening but you are watching something on the screen. Because you are removed – take the cameras back and you have that bird's eye view on what's been said rather than actually being part of the discussion. You are one step back from the discussion. (Clive)

When she steps back having seen herself on the DVD, Louisa recognises the point at which she is grappling with her own pathway forward. This decision-making in her professional learning illustrates her ownership of the process:

> I could see myself in the video thinking 'Oh oh oh what can I do next? What can I do next?' So it was really neat watching me think, just through that discussion, through that talk which that was really cool. (Louisa)

These 'thinking' comments illustrate the teachers' level of reflection on and in both their classroom practice and their coaching relationships. The use of the video as a revision tool for analysis of metacognition enabled the peer coaches to objectify their thinking. This visibility supported the teachers to think through the implications for their practice as they had a second look and a second think.

'Second look, second think'

Through their 'second look' at the recorded footage of their peer coaching collaborative dialogue, the teachers were able to have a 'second think' – making further meaning of their original thinking. By viewing this DVD footage the teachers could 'dig deeper' into their teacher inquiries. They had opportunities to think further and more deeply, affording additional insights as a result of this viewing.

Kay uses her computer to take notes as she views the DVD. She comments on how using the computer to manipulate her ideas assists her to think as she reviews the recorded footage. Through 'jotting things down' and 'cutting and pasting' her electronic notes, she makes sense of what she thinks. By jointly employing these two tools Kay clarifies her next-step actions:

> It was while I was watching the DVD … I was able to reach my goals during the interview with him better than last time. I felt that actually having the video and watching it and just jotting things down – I was cutting and pasting and moving things around [and] that actually clarified it for me and that's what I discussed in the interview. 'This is what I could do to make that happen.' So it was really good to have both parts of the process. (Kay)

Clive, like Kay, makes notes from the DVD. Clive reflects on what his colleague has said while reviewing the reflective dialogue and, as a consequence, determines his next step:

> It wasn't something I said. It was something Irene said. I wrote it down more or less, 'that the children don't understand that they are in charge of their learning.' – [It was] one of her little quotes and that was the point that I determined my next step. (Clive)

Kay also recognises a dissonance between the views she espouses on the DVD and her second think when she listens to what she had said. She objectifies herself and grounds her espoused theories in practice:

> … and I was disagreeing with myself on the DVD – like you would ask me something and I was sitting and I was going 'Oh yeah that happens' but when I was watching it I was thinking – 'No it doesn't actually.' (Kay)

Through reviewing the DVD, Kay identifies her next step. This is a second reflection opportunity for her and it triggers her memory. She highlights what she can do to improve the effectiveness of her teaching:

> It all came together sitting watching the DVD. Because [although] I did come up with a couple of extra steps I think on that day … what we talked [about] I forgot, you know. I was rushing off to the next thing. But sitting down watching the DVD it really brought it all together and highlighted a couple of areas that I really need to work on to improve the lessons for the kids in my room. (Kay)

Through his second look, Kevin reflects on the outcome of the peer coaching dialogue and realises that he has not followed through with his intended action. This has an impact on his awareness of his praxis at a meta-level as he realises that he needs to be more motivated:

> It's just trying to be able to get them. I think for me the point in the video where it really, really hit home for me was when we were talking about motivation and questions. I can't remember the exact dialogue what it was now, but I went away with a hiss and a roar as you do after and it petered out! That's when it clicked in for me – that I have to be more motivated for myself and for them. (Kevin)

Susan has a moment of realisation during the follow-up interview – she recognises the role of a colleague in activating her learning:

> I enjoyed it at the time having Kay there. But when I looked at the video I don't know that anything she said helped me to – Well, actually no! She was helping me reflect on this data, wasn't she? (Susan)

Kay sees the value of double reflection. By objectifying her thinking she sees the process more clearly:

> When you are watching yourself you can't see all the clutter in your head but when you are actually talking – [you are] trying to think and talk at the same time. (Kay)

Clive makes a new connection with his colleague's comments through having a fresh look. He rethinks his next step:

> Having another look at the video I made a connection with Ingrid's comment, which a lot of people say, 'Yeah – sure kids are always like that.' And then following on from that I just thought 'Well how *can* I do that' – how could I actually really. I guess that's the next step. (Clive)

Kay watches the video and, through seeing how her peer coach serves as a model to her, considers how she can model her thinking aloud, for her students:

> I thought after a while as I was watching the video of when we had that talk, my talk could therefore be maybe a model for the kids. If I'm thinking aloud then that could model to them how they could be thinking at the computers to work things through themselves. (Kay)

Susan, a school leader, talks about how the process of re-viewing the video enables her to identify additional ideas to follow-up with her colleague. She had not recognised these points while she was 'in the moment' during her initial peer coaching experience. This second look and think helps her in her leadership position to take actions in support of members of her team:

> It is very helpful watching the interview again 'cause you get something more – even [in] my conversation with Lynda – I went and had that time with her afterwards – [to] follow up with some of the points that had come up on the interview. But watching it again last night I thought 'Oh – I don't think we talked about [that]. I need to go back.' (Susan)

By watching the professional learning unfold on video, the teachers were afforded two layers of dialogic feedback. The initial coaching dialogue allowed for first-order feedback, and through later reviewing the DVD footage the teachers engaged in a second-order feedback process.

Conclusion

In a transformative model of CPD there is a recognition that teacher inquiry can be an empowering process and pre-prescribed solutions are not necessarily 'what works' across all contexts. In this research, video provided a mechanism that supported teachers' symbiotic feedback as a process of dialogic inquiry. This positioned teachers agentically in their learning. Through video, we were able to capture the workings of the intermediary liminal spaces between the teacher interlocutors. Deep teacher learning was afforded through this video-supported reflection and dialogue. Video, as conceptualised in this paper, is only useful in a CPD model that values teacher autonomy, where teachers drive the process. Therefore, the particular use of video as advocated here is model specific. This is a cautionary note for international CPD contexts.

The use of the DVD as a mediated tool enabled the teachers to ascend to a different level in their professional learning, to see their own process of reflection and extend their thinking further.

Our findings suggest that the use of video has the capacity to shape teacher professional learning. When used as a tool in conjunction with collaborative peer coaching it can raise teacher awareness on two levels. On one hand, there is the potential impact on classroom teaching as teachers build an understanding of their current practice and plan to enhance it as a result of their collaborative inquiries. On the other hand, videoed collaborative peer coaching can enhance teachers' peer coaching skills as they become explicitly aware of their own and others' processes of learning.

The teachers used video during the peer coaching to theorise and determine their next-step actions for their classroom practice. The video enabled them to surface and process what was subconscious or embedded in their thinking. The peer coaching supported a feedback process of critical reflection. During this reflective dialogue the teachers were 'in the moment'. However, when they stepped back to have a second look they were no longer group participants. Through viewing the DVD of themselves, the teachers noticed the complexities of their interactions with their peers and could reflect on their peer coaching. The teachers objectified their conversations, recognising their metacognitive processes. They reviewed the meanings they initially generated from their data. Through this collaborative approach the teachers surfaced what had been invisible, engaging in deep learning as they confronted what had been up until that moment subjective and in the dark.

Through enhancing their peer coaching skills the teachers instigated a mechanism for the ongoing development of sustainable practice. Dialogic feedback influenced the teachers' thinking and decision-making, and they became more explicitly aware of their peer coaching roles and their own professional learning processes. Teacher peer coaches noticed and recognised that this dialogic process supported their learning. Furthermore, the video afforded the teacher peer coaches a second chance to think about their thinking.

As a fresh way of using video, this supported the teachers' CPD. On its own, the mere presence of the video camera increased teacher self-awareness and focus, prompting the teachers to think about what sense an audience might be making when they subsequently view the DVD.

Through viewing video footage of the peer coaching, teachers built understandings of their dialogic relationships. These learning relationships appear to be integral to social inquiries where teachers engage in talk that is critical and challenging. The teachers were able to clarify their thinking through talking. They made connections with their peers' practices, scaffolding their ideas through the contributions of others. A collegial lens offered a liminal space in which the teachers thought about and co-constructed their practice. The teachers noted that their thinking was enhanced by this collaborative aspect.

Through viewing their video footage, the teachers were able to focus their thinking and therefore, through this second-look, second-think they constructed an additional layer of awareness. This opportunity for second-look, second-think has implications for models of continued professional development. Viewing the DVD reinforced the formation of the teachers' learning goals and supported their further thinking by the objectification of the initial reflective dialogue. This research recommends further exploration of dialogic practices that afford teachers opportunities to develop metacognitive awareness and an agentic role in their own learning. There is scope for further studies into the sustainability of this approach. This research raised the following further questions for us:

- How does dialogic peer coaching impact on teachers' classroom practice?
- How do peer coaching practices change after iterations of collaborative dialogic feedback?
- How can the use of information technologies in peer coaching support teacher metacognition and learner agency?
- What other technological innovations support a transformative model of teacher CPD?

The dialogic peer coaching approach as outlined in this paper honours the differing dispositions of participants and the contexts in which they work. Teachers are positioned agentically through their peer coaching experiences and have potential to self-transform. The process itself supported teachers to surface the invisible and critique their assumptions through critical reflection. The technology gave teachers ownership of their inquiries, enabling them to innovate in their teaching practice. The use of the video as a tool also enhanced teacher peer coaching skills. The research has implications for how leaders position teachers and how teachers position themselves and each other as agentic co-learners, activating learning in collaborative communities of inquiry.

References

Absolum, M., *et al.*, 2009. *Directions for assessment in New Zealand*. Wellington: Ministry of Education.

Alexander, R., 2005. Culture, dialogue and learning: notes on an emerging pedagogy. *In: International Association for Cognitive Education and Psychology (IACEP) 10th International Conference, Education, Culture and Cognition: intervening for growth*, 10–14 July, University of Durham, UK [online]. Available from: http://www.robinalexander. org.uk/docs/IACEP_paper_050612.pdf [Accessed 4 November 2011].

Askew, S. and Lodge, C., 2000. Gifts, ping pong and loops – linking feedback and learning. *In*: S. Askew, ed. *Feedback for learning*. London: Routledge Falmer, 1–17.

Bell, J., 2006. *Doing your research project. A guide for first-time researchers in education, health and social science*. Maidenhead: Open University Press.

Biesta, G., 2007. Why 'what works' won't work: evidence-based practice and the democratic deficit in educational research. *Educational theory*, 57 (1), 1–22.

Brookfield, S., 1995. *Becoming a critically reflective teacher*. San Francisco, CA: Jossey-Bass.

Carnell, E. and Lodge, C., 2002. *Supporting effective learning*. London: Paul Chapman.

Cohen, L., Manion, L., and Morrison, K., 2007. *Research methods in education*. 6th ed. London: RoutledgeFalmer.

Cutrim Schmid, E., 2011. Video-stimulated reflection as a professional development tool in interactive whiteboard research. *ReCALL*, 23 (3), 252–270.

Deakin Crick, R. and Joldersma, C., 2007. Habermas, lifelong learning and citizenship education. *Studies in philosophy and education*, 26 (2), 77–95.

Franz, N., 2007. Adult education theories: informing cooperative extension's transformation. *Journal of extension*, 45 (1) [online]. Available from: http://www.joe.org/joe/2007february/a1p.shtml [Accessed 4 November 2011].

Freed, S., 2003. Metaphors and reflective dialogue online. *New horizons in adult education*, 17 (3), 4–19.

Game, A. and Metcalfe, A., 2009. Dialogue and team teaching. *Higher education research and development*, 28 (1), 45–57.

Garvey Berger, J., 2002. Exploring the connection between teacher education practice and adult development theory. Unpublished doctoral dissertation, Harvard University Graduate School of Education, Cambridge, MA. Available from: http://www.cultivating-leadership.co.nz/wordpress/wp-content/uploads/2012/01/JG-Berger-Final-Dissertation.pdf [Accessed 8 November 2011].

Garvey Berger, J. 2006. *Key concepts for understanding the work of Robert Kegan* [online]. Available from: http://wiki.canterbury.ac.nz/download/attachments/6358104/Berger+Kegan+key+concepts+kb.doc?version=1 [Accessed 8 November 2011].

Kegan, R., 1994. *In over our heads: the mental demands of modern life*. Cambridge, MA: Harvard University Press.

Kegan, R. and Laskow, L., 2009. *Immunity to change: how to overcome it and unlock potential in yourself and your organization*. Boston, MA: Harvard Business School.

Kennedy, A., 2005. Models of continuing professional development: a framework for analysis. *Journal of in-service education*, 31 (2), 235–250.

Klenowski, V., 2009. Editorial: assessment for learning revisited: an Asia-Pacific perspective. *Assessment in education: principles, policy & practice*, 16 (3), 263–268.

Lincoln, Y. and Guba, E., 1985. *Naturalistic inquiry*. London: Sage.

Lom, E. and Sullenger, K., 2011. Informal spaces in collaborations: exploring the edges/boundaries of professional development. *Professional development in education*, 37 (1), 55–74.

McArdle, K. and Coutts, N., 2010. Taking teachers' continuous professional development beyond reflection: adding shared sense-making and collaborative engagement for professional renewal. *Studies in continuing education*, 32 (3), 201–215.

Mezirow, J., 1997. Transformative learning: theory to practice. *New directions for adult and continuing education*, 74, 5–12 [online]. Available from: http://www.hrdmax.com/images/column_1325932983/Mezirow%20Transformative%20Learning.pdf [Accessed 8 November 2011].

Ministry of Education, 2007. *The New Zealand curriculum*. Wellington: Government Printer.

Nehring, J., Laboy, W., and Catarius, L., 2010. Connecting reflective practice, dialogic protocols, and professional learning. *Professional development in education*, 36 (3), 399–420.

Orland-Barak, L., 2006. Convergent, divergent and parallel dialogues: knowledge construction in professional conversations. *Teachers and teaching: theory and practice*, 12 (1), 13–31.

Patton, M., 1990. *Qualitative evaluation and research methods*. 2nd ed. Newbury Park, CA: Sage.

Ravenscroft, A., Wegerif, R.B., and Hartley, J.R., 2007. Reclaiming thinking: dialectic, dialogic and learning in the digital age. *Special issue of British journal of educational psychology (BJEP): psychological insights into the use of new technologies in education*, 11 (5), 39–57.

Robbins, P., 1991. *How to plan and implement a peer coaching program*. Alexandria, VA: Association for Supervision and Curriculum Development.

Robertson, J., 2005. *Coaching leadership: building educational leadership capacity through coaching partnerships*. Wellington, New Zealand: NZCER Press.

Somerville, M., 2007. Postmodern emergence. *International journal of qualitative studies in education*, 20 (2), 225–243.

Sparks, D., 2005. *Leading for results: transforming teaching, learning, and relationships in schools*. Thousand Oaks, CA: Corwin Press.

Stover, K., *et al.*, 2011. Differentiated coaching: fostering reflection with teachers. *The reading teacher*, 64 (7), 498–509.

van Es, E., 2010. Viewer discussion is advised: video clubs focus teacher discussion on student learning. *Journal of staff development*, 31 (1), 54–70.

Wagenheim, G., Clark, R., and Crispo, A., 2009. Metaphorical mirror: reflecting on our personal pursuits to discover and challenge our teaching practice assumptions. *International journal of teaching and learning in higher education*, 20 (3), 503–509.

Watkins, C., 2000. Feedback between teachers. *In*: S. Askew, ed. *Feedback for learning*. London: Routledge Falmer, 65–80.

Wegerif, R., 2008. Dialogic or dialectic? The significance of ontological assumptions in research on educational dialogue. *British educational research journal*, 34 (3), 347–361.

Wiliam, D., 2006. Does assessment hinder learning? *Paper presented at the ETS Europe Breakfast Seminar*, 11 July, London [online]. Available from: http://www.decd.sa.gov. au/adelaidehills/files/links/williams_speec_1.pdf [Accessed 16 January 2013].

Wiliam, D., 2008. Changing classroom practice. *Educational leadership*, 65 (4), 36–42.

The 'trainer in your pocket': mobile phones within a teacher continuing professional development program in Bangladesh

Christopher S. Walsh[a], Tom Power[a], Masuda Khatoon[b], Sudeb Kumar Biswas[b], Ashok Kumar Paul[b], Bikash Chandra Sarkar[b] and Malcolm Griffiths[a]

[a]Department of Education, The Open University, Walton Hall, Milton Keynes, UK;
[b]English in Action, Dhaka, Bangladesh

Examples of mobile phones being used with teachers to provide continuing professional development (CPD) in emerging economies at scale are largely absent from the research literature. We outline English in Action's (EIA) model for providing 80,000 teachers with CPD to improve their communicative language teaching in Bangladesh over nine years. EIA's CPD program is delivered face to face and supported through open distance learning (ODL). This innovative model of teacher CPD is supported through peer learning and self-study using a variety of print, audio and video resources. Drawing on the success of EIA's pilot studies, where internal and external evaluation reported significant improvement in teachers' and students' English-language competence after one year, the current phase is using low-cost mobile phones, or the 'trainer in your pocket' to deliver CPD to 12,500 teachers through 2015. We believe EIA's teacher CDP model is best suited to assist the project in achieving one of its primary goals: to increase the English-language proficiency of 12 million students, allowing them to access greater social and economic opportunities in the future. We argue EIA's use of mobile phones for the provision of teacher CPD – at scale – is timely and replicable in both developed and developing contexts.

Introduction

The People's Republic of Bangladesh is one of the most densely populated countries in the world (United Nations Population Division 2007) and is largely monolingual. According to the Bangladesh Bureau of Educational Information and Statistics (BANBEIS 2003), Bengali or Bangla is the language of 95% of the population. This is in part due to the circumstances that led to the Bengali Language Movement, which later foreshadowed the Bengali nationalist movements and the Bangladesh Liberation War in 1971. The Language Movement had a major cultural impact on Bangladesh and this led to the celebration of Bangla language, literature and culture at the exclusion of other languages – particularly English – in the education system. In 1974 the Bangladesh Education Commission stated that no other language but Bangla should be taught during the primary years of schooling (classes one through five). It was not until 1990 that English became a compulsory subject from class one of primary schooling (Hoque 2009). As a result, the need for English teachers' continuing professional development (CPD) in Bangladesh is crucial for successful social and economic development into the future. Many current primary and secondary teachers, who had little or no experience with communicative English-language learning or teaching approaches, struggle with the communicative aspects of English, particularly speaking and listening.

Although a high poverty rate prevails in rural areas, the United Nations has commended Bangladesh for achieving remarkable progress in human development (United Nations Development Programme 2010). The present Government of Bangladesh fully recognizes the critical need to improve the quality of education alongside its efforts for creating equitable access to education (Rahman *et al.* 2010). Bangladesh has made significant improvement in providing more children and young people with access to education through increased enrolment, especially for girls. The country has also increased the number of schools and teachers, revised the primary and secondary English curriculum and published the national textbook *English for Today* (National Curriculum and Textbook Board 2003), used in all government schools, that encourages a communicative English teaching approach. Yet teaching English communicatively is inherently challenging because one in five teachers across the country have no teaching qualification (UIS 2006, Shohel and Banks 2010) and many English teachers use the grammar translation method of teaching. This method does not focus on teaching students how to communicate in English; rather, teachers 'translate' the text using Bangla focusing on reading and writing, rather than speaking and listening. Thus, comprehensive English teacher CPD that works at scale, and is sustainable into the future, is essential to ensure Bangladesh's continued economic growth by providing communicative English language as a tool for better access to the world economy.

This paper is presented in five sections. The first examines the literature on teachers' CPD and technology as well as the emerging use of mobile technologies for CPD and English-language teaching. The second section provides an overview of English in Action (EIA). It also outlines the results of EIA's first phase, baseline and pilot studies (2008–2011) and reports on the successes and challenges used to inform the project's current upscaling phase (2012–2015). The third section of the paper presents EIA's new mobile phone-based kit or 'trainer in your pocket' (Walsh 2011) that delivers communicative language teaching (CLT) audio and video CPD resources stored on micro secure digital (SD) cards. The fourth section of the paper outlines how the 'trainer in your pocket' is currently being used to provide 12,500 teachers with CPD (2012–2015) in EIA's model of school-based professional development (SBPD). This section exemplifies how EIA's SBPD model – with its use of low-cost mobile phones – has the potential to impact positively on more than 750,000 students in the next three years, helping them achieve higher levels of English-language proficiency. In conclusion, we argue EIA's model is a low-cost solution well suited to deliver teacher CPD at scale, which is timely and replicable for other developed and developing contexts.

Teachers' continuous professional development and technology

For more than a decade, the Internet has provided teachers with new opportunities for CPD because it provides multiple means for collaboration and reflection with other teachers and experts outside their schools (Hunter 2002). This makes it possible for teachers to interact with peers, and learn and access resources and guidance within a networked space (Bond 2004, Cornu 2004, Matei 2005) that is not bound by the constraints of the school day or academic year. The Vital program in England is one such example. It is a large-scale CPD program designed to enhance the teaching of information communication technology in state-funded primary and secondary schools. Vital's model encourages, extends and structures reflective practice and professional dialog, giving teachers time to embed new practices into their classrooms (Bradshaw *et al.* 2012). With a community of over 6000 teachers, Vital offers courses both online and with face-to-face support. Unique to Vital is how teachers can take a defined course of study and access resources, including the materials used in those courses. More significantly, Vital is built on the notion of a community of learners with pathways through learning. Teachers are seen as peers in the learning process rather than as recipients of professional development. Thus all registered users of Vital can upload and share resources, discuss ideas, take part in TeachShares and attend TeachMeets online (for more information, see Bradshaw *et al.* 2012).

An additional large-scale example of technology being harnessed for teachers' CPD is the UK Institute for Learning's program 'REfLECT', which is an online personal learning space for teachers. This enables teachers to plan, record and assess the impact of CPD on their practice. From 2008 to 2010, the number of teachers and trainers using REfLECT's 'personal space' to plan, record and review their CPD increased from 82,000 to over 106,000. Not surprising, increasingly REfLECT's members are reporting that they use mobile devices including mobile phones, tablets and personal digital assistants to capture the effects of CPD on themselves and others (Institute for Learning 2010).

Duncan-Howell's (2010) study also illustrates how teachers are increasingly using online communities for CPD, peer guidance, access to resources and inspiration. Her study investigated three online communities: one local Australian state-based community, one national Australian community and one international community. Duncan-Howell found that teachers who were participating in online communities spent one to three hours a week engaged in CPD because it was a form of participatory learning that focused on practical classroom strategies relevant to their teaching. All of these technology-based CPD initiatives work and are successful because they leverage the power of the Internet. But it is important to emphasize that these programs are generally online collaborative communities that use web-based discussion forums for knowledge and resource sharing (Wei and Chen 2006) in the *developed* world. In a context such as Bangladesh or other developing countries, where the majority of teachers cannot afford access to the Internet, similar teacher CPD initiatives remain impossible.

Mobile technologies for teachers' continuing professional development and English-language teaching

Mobile technologies, particularly mobile phones, for teacher CPD and English-language teaching and learning are still an emerging field in both developed and developing countries. There are many important case studies outside education that highlight the efficacy of mobile phones for entrepreneurial activity among women in Bangladesh (Aminuzzaman *et al.* 2003, Sullivan 2007), economic development in relation to microenterprises in Rwanda (Donner 2007), social innovations in health in Tanzania (Mulgan 2006) and India (Biswas *et al.* 2009), and activism (Zuckerman 2007). Important is leveraging the power of mobile phones, in similar ways, to provide effective and sustainable teacher CPD at scale.

There are few examples of educational projects using mobile phones to teach English. The studies that do exist are small in scale and generally provide examples of students using their own mobile phones to learn English (Thorton and Houser 2005, Cavus and Ibrahim 2009, Salameh 2011) or accessing programs on the Internet through their mobile phones for learning English (Ki Chune 2011). Cui and Wang (2008) outline the various ways mobile phones can be used to teach English as a foreign language. But their study, like many others, takes place in a developed country and is based on the notion that students have mobile phones. This is not the case in Bangladesh. Providing teacher CPD in a developing country at scale is a unique challenge if it is to have similar successful outcomes to those reported on in the literature from the developing world. In what follows we outline EIA, arguably the world's largest English teacher CPD program, which is currently (2012) providing 4500 teachers with a robust CPD program that leverages the power of low-cost mobile phones to change English teaching and learning for 300,000 students.

English in Action

The importance of learning English to improve the social and economic prospects of all Bangladeshis – particularly those living in poverty – has become a government priority. As a result, EIA was launched in 2008 to significantly increase the number of people able to communicate in English to levels that enable them to participate more fully in economic and social opportunities. EIA is a nine-year (2008–2017) language education program that strives to develop the communicative English language skills of 25 million Bangladeshis. The project is funded by UKaid from the Department for International Development (DfID) and works closely with the Government of Bangladesh's Ministry of Primary and Mass Education (MoPME) and the Ministry of Education.

EIA's primary project goal is to contribute to the economic growth of Bangladesh by providing communicative English language as a tool for better access to the world economy. The project consists of a consortium of partners working together: BMB Mott MacDonald, BBC Media Action (previously BBC World Service Trust), The Open University, UK and two Bangladeshi non-governmental organizations – the Underprivileged Children's Educational Program and Friends in Village Development Bangladesh. The consortium partners bring unique expertise in specialized areas to ensure a collective effort in achieving the project's goals. BBC Media Action is providing a diversity of programs aimed at improving 13 million adult learners' communicative English language skills.[1] This paper focuses on EIA's provision of an innovative school-based professional development (SBPD) program using mobile phones to improve 12 million students' communicative English-language skills from 2012 to 2017.

EIA's work is closely aligned with the democratic government of Bangladesh's Prime Minister's Office's philosophy of 'Digital Bangladesh'. The philosophy of 'Digital Bangladesh' is an attempt to ensure the citizens of Bangladesh's democracy and rights. It aims to be transparent, accountable, establish justice and ensure the delivery of government services through the widespread use of technology to improve the lives of Bangladeshis regardless of class or social status. EIA's innovative teacher CPD approach, firmly situated within existing government initiatives, will provide teacher professional development at scale to 80,000 teachers by 2017 using mobile phones through open distance learning (ODL) with audio and video resources on 4 GB micro SD cards. The program also supplies teachers with supplementary print teacher guides and visual resources for both primary and secondary English teachers.

English in Action's developmental research, baseline and pilot studies

EIA's developmental research, baseline and pilot studies were carried out with 700 teachers from government schools across 21 of Bangladesh's *upazilas* (sub-districts), as well as some 60 teachers from non-governmental organizations (2008–2011). Two-thirds of these teachers work in primary schools, one-third in secondary schools. Eighty percent of all EIA pilot study schools are in rural areas with limited or no access to electricity. The developmental research, baseline and pilot studies helped the project explore the use of mobile technologies for English teachers' CPD and the delivery of audio resources for classroom use.

EIA's pilot studies (2009–2010) provided extensive audio and visual resources to primary and secondary English teachers on the Apple iPod Touch (for primary teachers) and iPod Nano (for secondary teachers) with portable rechargeable speakers. The iPods assisted teachers in learning and trying out new CLT practices with their students. Importantly, these MP3 players also provided primary teachers with audio resources specifically produced to match every lesson in the national textbook series *English for Today* for grades one through five. This gave teachers and students examples of Bangladeshis speaking textbook content in English. The voices were not native English speakers, but clearly Bangladeshi individuals speaking English in an entirely communicative manner. In total, each primary teacher received 355 audio files that were primarily dialogs that matched the lessons in each of the five primary national textbooks. The iPod Nanos also provided primary teachers with songs for the beginning and end of every lesson, and a range of supplementary songs, poems and dialogs. In addition, all primary teachers received EIA-produced Activity Guides at each of the five grade levels with complementary visual (posters, flash cards, figurines) and print resources (audio transcripts of the dialogs). For primary teachers' CPD, the iPod Nanos also included 18 video clips and four audio recordings that exemplify a range of correct and incorrect English CLT classroom practices.

Secondary teachers received fewer additional classroom resources because they generally have higher levels of English-language proficiency and have received more pedagogical training. To support CLT practices in the secondary classroom, teachers were provided with lesson plan cards, maps, and photographs. The secondary teachers were also supplied with 46 audio files dedicated to teacher CPD on the iPod Touch. The secondary teachers' iPod Touch was preloaded with audio podcasts enhanced with synchronized text and images as well as 12 CPD videos. This was the core of their teacher CPD materials. They also received a print-based teacher professional development package entitled *English for Today in Action*, which presents 12 CLT modules to use with the accompanying 12 CPD videos (active listening, predictive listening, using visual aids, creative writing, role-play, etc.) that they can learn from, adapt and use to teach communicative English. EIA's pilot study provided the CPD materials on the iPods for teachers to use for self-study to learn new CLT practices. The CPD videos illustrated the incorrect (videos had a red 'x' in the lower-right-hand corner) and correct (videos had a green check in the lower-right-hand corner) ways to introduce and implement CLT activities in their English classroom.

The iPods were chosen because the project believed the teachers would find the use of the Apple MP3 players relatively easy. Although iPods were more expensive than other devices, they were chosen because they had the functionalities the project believed necessary to provide teacher CPD through ODL. They were also chosen because they made it easy to deliver classroom-based audio resources the project produced that were aligned with the national textbook. These crucial resources played on portable rechargeable speakers were essential for improving the communicative English proficiencies of both students and teachers. Internal and external research, monitoring and evaluation were carried out in order to explore the successes and challenges of using the iPods to deliver teacher CPD and classroom audio resources. These studies indicated that both primary and secondary teachers and students participating in the project found the use of the iPods and portable speakers an effective and successful tool for learning communicative English. On interview teachers also reported the audio and video CPD resources were beneficial and helped them learn and experiment with new CLT practices in their classroom.

Pilot study results and challenges

EIA conducts internal and external research, monitoring and evaluation activities as a requirement to the UK's Department for International Development (DfID). Before the pilot study, to better understand the unique context of Bangladesh, EIA conducted six baseline studies to identify the contexts in which the project was beginning (2009). This included: large-scale examinations of teachers' classroom practice; teachers' and students' competence in speaking and listening in English; students' and communities' attitudes and motivations towards English-language learning; the materials and training programs currently used in Bangladesh for teaching and learning English; and the communications technologies and power supplies used and/or available within schools and communities.[2]

After the pilot study, EIA conducted a large-scale quantitative study entitled 'The Classroom Practices of Primary and Secondary School Teachers Participating in English in Action' (EIA 2011). The study researched the extent of changes in the classroom practices of teachers participating in EIA after one year. One lesson from 350 primary teachers and 141 of the secondary teachers were observed. The results were compared with those observed in the 2009 baseline studies prior to the intervention. The 2011 study found a marked increase in the amount of student talk in lessons, as well as an increase in the use of English by both teachers and students across primary and secondary classrooms.

Remarkably, the 2011 study indicates that when primary teachers were talking, they used English 71% of the time. This marks a pronounced increase from an earlier baseline study where only 27% of teachers spoke in English more than they did in Bangla. The amount of time primary students were talking in English rose from 4% in the baseline study to 88% after one year of participating in EIA. Observations also indicate that students were engaged in communicative learning activities where they were either speaking in chorus (40%), talking on their own (30%), talking as part of pair work (14%) or speaking in group work (16%). The study also reported similar results for secondary teachers and students. When secondary students were talking, they used English 88% of the time. Thirty-nine percent of the time they were talking on their own, but they were also frequently engaged in both pair (31% of the time) and group work (26% of the time).

This 2011 study of the pilot phase indicates significant changes in classroom practices and the amount of English used as a result of participating in EIA's teacher CPD program. In the baseline studies, teachers observed were primarily reading from the textbook, rarely involving students in activities, and roughly 70% of the teachers were speaking English less than Bangla. In only a small percentage of lessons observed in the baseline studies did the students speak in English, or have opportunities to participate actively by answering questions or engaging in group or pair work.

External research, monitoring and evaluation

Trinity College externally evaluated the project using the Trinity Graded Examinations in Spoken English (Trinity College London 2007). Each interviewee's spoken English was evaluated against the criteria of the 12-point Trinity College English Language scale. Grade 1 represents very little spoken English competence and Grade 12 indicates complete competence. The grades are sub-divided into four stages: initial (Grades 1–3); elementary (Grades 4–6); intermediate (Grades 7–9); and advanced (Grades 10–12). In 2010, Trinity assessors used questionnaires to assess 4630 primary and 2609 secondary students' English-language competence before their teachers participated in EIA's CPD program. Then in 2011, Trinity assessed 786 primary and 318 secondary students from the 2010 cohort. For primary students, prior to the teachers' participation in EIA, 64.3% of students failed to pass Trinity's graded examination. In 2011, this number dropped to 49.9%. In 2010, 35.4% of the students scored initial (passing) levels of English-language competency, and this number rose to 50.1% in 2011. In secondary students, while the proportion of students who failed (below Grade 1) dropped from 28.9% to 10.4% in 2011, the number of students who passed at the initial levels (Grades 1–3) rose from 61.9% to 66.6%. Students passing at the elementary level (Grades 4–6) rose from 9.2% to 22.4%, a considerable increase. Both internal and external evaluation of the pilot study indicates EIA's teacher CPD and the use of the iPods were successful at encouraging higher percentages of teachers and students to speak English in the classroom. Additionally, the Trinity research indicates that teachers and students acquired higher levels of communicative (speaking and listening) English-language competency after participating in the project.

Challenges

Although the pilot phase was successful in terms of the iPods used for teachers' CPD, there were considerable challenges reported. A significant challenge was that many teachers found it very difficult to charge both the iPod and speaker due to the intermittent availability of electricity across Bangladesh. The project did notice that teachers prioritized the charging of their personal mobile phones over the iPods and speakers. On interview, teachers often reported that it was onerous and time-consuming to charge two additional devices. Another challenge was the size of the speakers chosen for the pilot study. For some teachers, it was difficult to transport the speakers home or to a location to charge them. There were other challenges too, but these were less critical. For example, some teachers did experience difficulty in finding files on the iPods to match their lessons in the national textbooks. The most significant challenge the project encountered was the high cost of the iPod Nano and Touch. These MP3 players are too expensive to provide to 12,500 teachers in the current upscaling phase (2012–2015).

As a result, the project needed to rethink what was not only possible but also sustainable into the future. This led to a smaller technology kit pilot study (2011) that used the same set of materials on two low-cost mobile phones with 4 GB micro SD cards and smaller portable rechargeable speakers. The pilot study proved extremely successful, and in what follows we describe how the new mobile phone-based technology kit or 'trainer in your pocket' is being used in EIA's model of CPD for English teachers at scale.

The 'trainer in your pocket'

EIA understands, from internal research, their pilot studies and what exists in the literature, that mobile technologies offer increased opportunities by providing more choice in when, where and how teachers teach and how students learn. Unlike many other funded international development projects specific to mobile phones and often driven on making the various technologies work to ensure learning happens and satisfies funding conditions in the present, EIA has been conceptualized to intentionally address issues of scale, embedding and quality for the present and future across rural and urban contexts. Budget constraints of 6000 Bangladeshi Taka (£60) per teacher mandated that EIA construct multiple kits to field test and pilot the use of the 'trainer in your pocket' idea for the current upscaling phase (2012–2015), while also thinking post-2015 when there will be much less funding available for the approximately 67,500 teachers to whom EIA will still be required to provide a program of CPD. As result of the field test of the two low-cost mobile phones and 4 GB micro SD cards and portable rechargeable speakers from March to September (2011) in two rural *upazilas*, EIA designed a new technology kit that has been distributed to 4500 teachers (June–December 2012) across Bangladesh. The kit consists of the Nokia C1–01 (£35) mobile phone, a portable rechargeable Lane amplifier (£25) and all of EIA's CPD materials and classroom audio resources on 4 GB micro SD cards (£2).

All of EIA's CPD materials were revised for use with the new mobile phone-based 'trainer in your pocket'. Primary and secondary teachers received the new technology kit and an EIA-produced teacher guide. Separate teacher guides were authored and produced for both primary and secondary teachers. Additionally, guides were also produced for teacher facilitators whose role is to train the teachers in the project. Each primary and secondary teacher guide contains eight modules to be used over a 16-month cycle of SBPD. Teachers' mobile phones have a number of videos that are used in tandem with each of the eight modules in the guide to explain different CLT pedagogies (using a narrator), illustrate new English CLT teaching and learning practices (using EIA teachers and students who participated in the pilot studies) and prompt teachers to try similar activities in their classrooms.

The narrator introduces the activities in Bangla (for the primary teachers) and then a video is shown illustrating the CLT practices in a real Bangladeshi classroom using EIA audio or visual resources. Afterwards, the narrator comes back on to explain what the teachers have just viewed in the video and encourages teachers to 'try it' (similar activities) in their classroom. For the secondary teachers, the format is the same but it is primarily in English with less Bangla.

To understand how the 'trainer in your pocket' works for teacher CPD we will illustrate an example from the EIA-produced *Secondary Teacher Guide: Secondary Teaching and Learning* from Module 7 on 'Speaking'. In the Secondary Teacher Guide, there are places in the module that direct the teachers to watch a video on their mobile phone. For Module 7, there are three video clips, four audio files and a 'Teachers Talking' audio file. In the first video clip, the narrator introduces the module (Figure 1):

> Hello and welcome to Module 7 which focuses on freer speaking activities. We begin with part 1 SM7-V1, 'Using dialogues for speaking practice'. In Module 3 you saw a teacher getting his student to repeat a dialogue. In the video clip you are about to watch you see a different teacher doing another dialogue from Class 6, this time Unit 7, Lesson 6. The students have practiced repeating the dialogue as a whole class and now they are repeating the dialogue in pairs. This is to help them feel more familiar and more confident with the language. Watch the video clip and note down what the teacher does when the students have finished repeating the dialogues in pairs.

Then there is a video of the classroom that the teachers need to watch (Figure 2). The video starts with the students practicing dialogs and the teacher writing questions on the board. The teacher then models a dialog with a student at the front of the class using questions on the board. Then he asks two student volunteers to come to the front of the class and perform the dialog using the questions on the blackboard as a scaffold. Afterwards, students are asked to practice in pairs. There are over 60 students in the classroom, with male and female students sitting on opposite sides of the classroom.

The camera focuses in on students talking in pairs. Afterwards the narrator comes back on and says:

Figure 1. The EIA narrator introducing a lesson.

Figure 2.   An example of the teacher using CLT technique introduced by the narrator.

So what did the teacher do when the students finished repeating the dialogue in pairs? First of all the teacher asked for a volunteer from the class and then he asked the student some key questions from the dialogue. But the student did not repeat the answers from the dialogue from the *English for Today* textbook. The student gave real answers. She gave the real date and the real date of her birthday. By the way, did you notice that the teacher had written these key questions on the board? He did this while the students were practicing the dialogue in pairs. After this, the teacher asked for two more volunteers. The students asked each other questions using the prompts on the board. And once again the students gave real answers. The dialogue is now different from the one in the *English for Today* textbook.

Did you notice that the teacher didn't correct the students when they were talking? Why do you think he didn't correct them? This conversation is to help students practice talking about dates, but the teacher is also trying to get students to talk more extensively, to communicate with each other in a real way. Students need opportunities to practice speaking more freely like this if they are to practice speaking more fluently in English. That is with confidence and without hesitation. When students talk more freely, they will make more mistakes, but if the teacher corrects each mistake, then the students will lose confidence and won't feel very motivated to speak. Now that the students have seen two examples of a conversation, one by the teacher and a student, the other by two students, the students are ready to do the same in pairs. They understand what language they need to use and understand what they need to do.

Working in pairs means that all of the students get an opportunity to speak some English. As they do the activity, the teacher walks around and listens to the students. When the students finish, the teacher can give the class some feedback on common problems many of the students had. For example perhaps the students forgot to use 'the' when saying a date. This will be a helpful reminder for the students when they come to the next exercise in the *English for Today* textbook. There are many dialogues in the *English for Today* textbooks that your students could act out and use as a model for their own conversations. In the next part of this module you will learn more about how to do this in the classroom. Now go to Module 7, 'Try it in the classroom 1' and learn more about acting out dialogues in the classroom.

This illustrates how the 'trainer in your pocket' is used in the cluster meetings and for self-study through ODL. Paramount to this form of teacher CPD is the fact that teachers can go back and revisit the videos and actually see the CLT practices working in real Bangladeshi classrooms similar to their own. The additional audio clips are often of useful phrases to use in the classroom and the 'Teachers Talking' audio files are a group of teachers answering common questions which the teachers are asked to answer themselves at the end of each module.

Importantly, both primary and secondary teachers also receive *English Language for Teachers* (EL4T), an English for Specific Purposes self-study program that has 30 lessons with 30 accompanying audio files. The purpose of these CPD materials is to develop teachers' communicative English in the areas of reading, writing, speaking and listening. EL4T focuses on English functional language, structures and vocabulary of direct relevance to classroom teaching and Bangladesh's national textbook series, *English for Today*. There are 30 lessons for primary teachers and then an additional 30 lessons for secondary teachers that present and reflect the CLT pedagogy that underpins EIA's CPD program. Additionally there are BBC Media Action self-study CPD materials on pronunciation (25 self-study audio files) and vocabulary (38 self-study audio files) included on the micro SD card. Taken together, all of these audio and video resources stored on 4 GB micro SD cards make EIA's 'trainer in your pocket' a remarkable low-cost tool for providing teacher CPD at scale.

English in Action's model of school-based professional development (SBPD) for English teachers

EIA's SBPD model for teacher CPD assists teachers in learning and applying their communicative English-language teaching practices in the classrooms, schools and communities where they work. Through supported ODL using the 'trainer in your

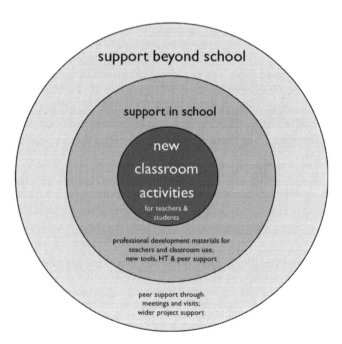

Figure 3. EIA's SBPD model to support changes in classroom practice (Walsh and Power 2011).

pocket', the classroom becomes the nexus of learning. With EIA's model, teachers are not left alone to make sense of the ODL materials. Rather, they engage with the materials while receiving support from a teacher-partner within their school, a community of teacher colleagues from their *upazilas* and through bi-monthly cluster meetings over the course of 16 months. This unique program, illustrated in Figure 3, helps teachers to develop, support and sustain new English CLT practices that are student-centered and markedly different from the kind of teaching and learning that was observed in the 2009 baseline studies.

With EIA's model of teacher professional development, participation in new classroom activities is at the center of teachers' CPD. These activities consist of the new CLT practices they are embodying after engaging with the teacher CPD materials on their mobile phones and in cluster meetings. There are two additional layers of support that enable teachers to carry out these new activities. The first layer of support is always 'on hand' and in school. The second layer is beyond the school. 'Support in school' includes the bank of audio resources directly aligned with the national textbooks. These audio files are introduced sequentially and a narrator always introduces each lesson by saying *'English for Today*, Class 1, Lesson 1', ensuring that both teachers and students know the audio explicitly goes with a particular lesson in the national textbook. The narrator often speaks in Bangla to help students understand what they are going to listen to. Each of EIA's audio lessons is designed to be used over two to three days with lessons. In total there are currently 452 audio lessons for the primary classroom. There are 190 audio lessons for the secondary classroom including recordings of stories, dialogs, passages and poems for classes six through ten and the lessons in *English for Today*. Additional support in school is provided by the head teachers, who also receive EIA CPD materials and attend separate cluster meetings over 16 months that are specifically designed to help them encourage teachers to both engage in CPD and try the new CLT activities in their school. Peer support is also always on hand, because two teachers from each selected school attend the 16-month cycle of EIA's SBPD. 'Support beyond the school' consists of peer support, cluster meetings and wider project support including school visits and knowledge sharing.

Towards sustainable teacher continuing professional development at scale

EIA's model of SBPD and the 'trainer in your pocket' is assisting teachers to learn and apply their communicative English-language learning in the classrooms, schools and communities where they work – at scale. Presently 4500 teachers are participating in the 16-month course of CPD and every teacher has the suite of audio and visual resources on the Nokia C1–01 mobile phone or 'trainer in your pocket'. The project anticipates results similar to, or better than, those reported on in the pilot study and external evaluation in the current upscaling phase.

EIA's teacher professional development program will support 80,000 teachers in working collaboratively to initiate, trial and reflect upon new English CLT practices with the goal of adapting and embodying these strategies in their professional practice through 2017. They will continue to be supported in this by their peers (in school, and in local networks inside and beyond their school), and through the materials (print, audio and visual) and tools (mobile phones) provided. This is because it is not a model of teacher CPD that is delivered through traditional ODL (self-study), nor is it traditional teacher training in which the training and support is offered at a center that is physically and conceptually 'distant' from the teachers' context of practice – their classroom. Rather, it is dynamic, generative and leverages teachers' use of their mobile phones by providing numerous high-quality audio and video resources that can be used for self-study and English classroom teaching regardless of time, place or location.

We argue that incorporating mobile phones within a robust teacher CPD program like the one described in this paper presents unprecedented opportunities for hundreds of thousands of teachers and millions of students to acquire English – to levels that enable them to participate more fully in economic and social opportunities. We have observed existing classroom contexts in remote areas and have demonstrated the potential of using EIA's resources on mobile phones with lightweight portable speakers. This highlights how mobile phones, as a tool, can change learning and even individuals' livelihoods.

Importantly, EIA is not relying on the Internet or the network aspect of mobile phones which characterizes digitized aspects of some teacher CPD in the developed world. Rather, its teacher CPD resources fit onto a 4 GB micro SD card that currently costs less than £2. In 2015, when the project begins its third phase – the institutionalization phase – the cost of this technology will be even cheaper. It is anticipated that the final phase of EIA's project will design a flexible and institutionalized model that will enable the Government of Bangladesh, non-governmental organizations and community-based organizations to implement EIA's innovative model themselves and on a continuous basis. To realize this, EIA's approaches and materials are also currently being embedded into the Government of Bangladesh's National Academy for Primary Education's (Nape) Diploma in Education program (DipEd). This new DipEd will introduce EIA's CLT classroom practices using EIA's audio and visual materials within a highly practical and intensive two-year initial training program that emphasizes reflection and extensive practical experience in schools.

Starting in 2012, pre-service teachers will be trained using EIA's approaches, and by 2014 they are expected to start entering primary schools each subsequent year already familiar with the CLT approaches EIA currently provides to in-service teachers through its SBPD model. Introducing these new pedagogical approaches at scale in initial training alongside the current EIA in-service SBPD model will not only embed the project in existing government programs, but will also provide greater chances of sustainability. This step towards institutionalization has two important advantages. First, there will be a larger critical mass of English teachers equipped to teach English using communicative language approaches. Secondly, the DipEd goes far beyond English-language teaching and covers all primary school subjects. This means there is a high probability that EIA's student-centered pedagogical approaches in other subjects besides English may also have a sustainable impact. Significantly, embedding the DipEd within a number of teacher training colleges and pedagogical training institutes provides unforeseen opportunities to mainstream and institutionalize EIA's innovative practices at higher levels in the educational hierarchy.

In addition to the DipEd, EIA hopes to continue to make a large impact on English-language teaching and learning after the end of the project in 2017, with as many educational service providers and teachers as possible. To make EIA's model and classroom audio resources and CPD materials sustainable, EIA is currently planning on making all of the project's materials open educational resources

(OERs). Turning all EIA materials into OERs will make this model of teacher CPD and the accompanying resources freely available to teacher educators and teachers across Bangladesh and the globe. Feedback from the 4500 teachers already using the 'trainer in your pocket' is impressive and inspiring. The Nokia C1–01 mobile phones and micro SD cards are proving to be an excellent choice to deliver both the teacher CPD and classroom audio resources. Without being overly presumptuous, drawing on the success of the pilot studies and current feedback from the 4500 teachers using 'the trainer in your pocket' with over 300,000 students, we argue that EIA's model is a low-cost solution well suited to deliver teacher CPD at scale, which is timely and replicable for other developed and developing contexts.

Notes

1. For more information, see http://www.bbc.co.uk/mediaaction/search?term=English+in+Action+.
2. To view the baseline studies, see http://www.eiabd.com/eia/index.php?option=com_content&view=article&id=160&Itemid=61.

References

Aminuzzaman, S., Baldersheim, H., and Jamil, I., 2003. Talking back! Empowerment and mobile phones in rural Bangladesh: a study of the village phone scheme of Grameen Bank. *Contemporary south Asia*, 12 (3), 327–348.

BANBEIS, 2003. *Bangladesh bureau of educational information and statistics*. Dhaka: Ministry of Education.

Biswas, R., *et al.*, 2009. Revitalizing primary health care and family medicine/primary care in India – disruptive innovation? *Journal of evaluation in clinical practice*, 15 (5), 873–880.

Bond, P., 2004. Communities of practice and complexity: conversation and culture. *Organisations and people*, 11 (4), 1–7.

Bradshaw, P., Twining, P., and Walsh, C.S., 2012. The vital program: transforming ICT professional development. *American journal of distance education*, 26 (2), 74–85.

Cavus, N. and Ibrahim, D., 2009. M-Learning: an experiment in using SMS to support learning new English language words. *British journal of educational technology*, 40 (1), 78–91.

Cornu, B., 2004. Networking and collecting intelligence for teachers and learners. *In*: A. Brown and N. Davis, eds. *Digital technology, communities and education*. London: Routledge, 40–45.

Cui, G. and Wang, S., 2008. Adopting cell phones in EFL teaching and learning. *Journal of educational technology development and exchange*, 1 (1), 69–80.

Donner, J., 2007. The use of mobile phones by microentrepreneurs in Kigali, Rwanda: changes to social and business networks. *Information technologies and international development*, 3 (2), 3–19.

Duncan-Howell, J., 2010. Teachers making connections: online communities as a source of professional learning. *British journal of educational technology*, 41 (2), 324–340.

English in Action, 2011. *The classroom practices of primary and secondary school teachers participating in English in Action*. Dhaka, Bangladesh: EIA. Available from: http://www.eiabd.com/eia/research-reports/Research%20Report.pdf [Accessed 1 July 2012].

Hoque, S., 2009. Teaching English in primary schools in Bangladesh: competencies and achievements. *In*: J. Enever, J. Moon, and U. Raman, eds. *Young learner English language policy and implementation: international perspectives*. Reading, UK: Garnet Education, 61–69.

Hunter, B., 2002. Learning in the virtual community depends upon changes in local communities. *In*: K.A. Renninger and W. Shumar, eds. *Building virtual communities*. Cambridge: Cambridge University Press, 96–126.

Institute for Learning, 2010. *2009–10 IfL review of CPD excellence in professional development: looking back, looking forward*. London, UK: Institute for Learning.

Ki Chune, N., 2011. Optimising the use of wireless application protocol (WAP) sites for listening activities in a Korean English as a foreign language (EFL) context. *Computer assisted language learning*, 24 (2), 103–116.

Matei, S.A., 2005. *From counterculture to cyberculture: virtual community discourse and the dilemma of modernity* [online]. Available from: http://jcmc.indiana.edu/vol10/issue3/matei.html [Accessed 1 July 2012].

Mulgan, G., 2006. The process of social innovation. *Innovations: technology, governance, globalization*, 1 (2), 145–162.

National Curriculum and Textbook Board, 2003. *National curriculum and textbook board*. Dhaka, Bangladesh: Ministry of Education.

Rahman, M.M.R., *et al*., 2010. Historical development of secondary education in Bangladesh: colonial period to 21st century. *International education studies*, 3 (1), 114–125.

Salameh, O., 2011. A multimedia offline cell phone system for English language learning. *International Arab journal of e-technology*, 2 (1), 44–48.

Shohel, M.M.C. and Banks, F., 2010. Teachers' professional development through the English in Action secondary teaching and learning program in Bangladesh: experience from the UCEP schools. *Procedia social and behavioral sciences*, 2 (2), 5494–5843.

Sullivan, N.P., 2007. *Can you hear me now? How microloans and cell phones are connecting the world's poor to the global economy*. San Francisco, CA: Jossey-Bass.

Thorton, P. and Houser, C., 2005. Using mobile phones in English education in Japan. *Journal of computer assisted learning*, 21 (3), 217–228.

Trinity College London, 2007. *Graded examinations in spoken English 2007_2010* [online]. Available from: http://www.trinitycollege.co.uk/resource/?id_1487 [Accessed 1 July 2012].

UIS, 2006. *Teachers and educational quality: monitoring global needs for 2015*. Montreal: UNESCO Institute for Statistics.

United Nations Development Program, 2010. *Human development report 2010, The real wealth of nations: pathways to human development* [online]. United Nations. Available from: http://hdr.undp.org/en/reports/global/hdr2010/chapters/ [Accessed 1 July 2012].

United Nations Population Division, 2007. *World population prospects: the 2004 revision, analytical report, Volume III, the department of economic and social affairs* [online]. Available from: www.un.org/esa/population/unpop.htm [Accessed 1 July 2012].

Walsh, C.S., 2011. E-learning in Bangladesh: the 'trainer in your pocket' [online]. *In*: M.B. Nunes and M. McPherson, eds. *IADIS International Conference e-Learning 2011, a part of the IADIS Multi Conference on Computer Science and Information Systems 2011, 20–23 July 2011*. Rome, Italy: IADIS Press, 165–172. Available from: http://sep.mdu.edu.tw/ezfiles/0/1000/academic/37/academic_7118_1127959_92557.pdf [Accessed 1 December 2012].

Walsh, C.S. and Power, T., 2011. Rethinking development and the use of mobile technologies: lessons from Bangladesh. *In*: S.-M. Barton, J. Hedberg, and K. Suzuki, eds. *Proceedings of Global Learn 40 Asia Pacific 2011*, 2163–2172.

Wei, F. and Chen, G., 2006. Collaborative mentor support in a learning context using a ubiquitous discussion forum to facilitate knowledge sharing for lifelong learning. *British journal of educational technology*, 37 (6), 917–935.

Zuckerman, E., 2007. *Draft paper on mobile phones and activism* [online]. Available from: http://www.worldchanging.com/archives/006458.html [Accessed 1 July 2012].

Professional learning to support elementary teachers' use of the iPod Touch in the classroom

Katia Ciampa and Tiffany L. Gallagher

Teacher Education Department, Brock University, St. Catharines, Ontario, Canada

This single case study reports on the programme of professional learning that a Canadian staff of elementary teachers (Junior Kindergarten to Grade Eight) and their school principal engaged in to learn to use a mobile multimedia device as an instructional resource. The professional learning was facilitated by two university researchers who used the gradual release of responsibility framework to work with the teachers' attitudes about using iPod Touches and their need for technological pedagogical content knowledge. Fourteen teachers co-planned and co-taught technology-enhanced lessons during a five-month period. This study proposes a framework that outlines particular characteristics for supporting elementary teachers' effective integration of mobile multimedia technology into classroom practice. The school principal's role as a leader of technological change is highlighted along with the facilitators' roles as coaches as the teachers began to gradually embrace the multimedia technology as an instructional resource.

Introduction

Curriculum guidelines from the Ontario Ministry of Education include interwoven objectives for information technology. Teachers are compelled to integrate computer technology into their teaching in all grades and in all subject areas (Ministry of Education of Ontario 2007). The school site featured in this research owned a set of 30 iPod Touches, but these devices were not being utilised. It was rationalised that the capacity of the teachers to use this technology in their daily classroom instruction had not kept pace with the increased access to the technology (Druin 2009) and that a lack of teacher confidence in using the technology contributed to its instructional potential not being realised (Sandholtz 2001).

The iPod Touch is a small, mobile multimedia player with a touch-sensitive screen that provides the user with access to applications, videos, audio, photographs, documents and the Internet (Banister 2010). According to Banister (2010), this mobile device is equipped to perform a multitude of complex tasks, many of which can be used to accomplish a myriad of educational objectives in such curricular areas as reading, mathematics, social studies and science. Because the iPod

Touch is mobile, teachers and students can access content 'anytime, anywhere'. The iPod touch is viewed as a tool for delivering differentiated, autonomous and individualised instruction through mobile devices, which is especially important for students performing below grade level (Banister 2010). Many iPod apps allow for differentiated instruction because of the apps' setting features. For example, teachers can customise learning content to specific curricular and individual student needs, and adjust the length of the timer as well as the number of problems to present (Banister 2010). The iPod also makes it easy for teachers to provide textual, auditory and visual resources to reach all types of learners (Banister 2010).

Meaningful technology use in the K–8 classroom presents an ongoing challenge in education. With few exceptions, most professional development programmes for teachers in the area of technology integration have solely focused on the technology itself and software (Lawless and Pellegrino 2007). However, providing technical skills training to teachers in the use of technology is not enough. Teachers also need professional development in the pedagogical application of those skills to improve teaching and learning (Carlson and Gadio 2002). One of the most effective ways to help teachers take advantage of and integrate technology into their classroom instruction is to provide situated professional development, consisting of hands-on technology use, onsite mentorship, just-in-time support that addresses teachers' needs, individualised instruction, observation of technology integration in practice and self-directed learning (Jacobsen 2001, 2002). This approach goes beyond techno-centric strategies (teaching the tool) and emphasises the importance of helping teachers develop and apply understandings of technology, curriculum content and specific pedagogical approaches that support successful technology-enhanced teaching (teaching with the tool; Mishra and Koehler 2006).

The concept of Technological Pedagogical Content Knowledge (TPACK) offers a framework for investigating the skills and knowledge involved in integrating technology into teaching and classroom instruction (Koehler and Mishra 2009). TPACK considers teachers' knowledge as complex and multifaceted, critiquing techno-centric approaches that solely focus on the attainment of technology skills separate from pedagogy and content (Koehler and Mishra 2009). According to Koehler and Mishra (2009), TPACK is an understanding that emerges from an interaction of technology, pedagogy and content knowledge. Such a conceptualisation implies that teachers must engage with technology, pedagogy and content in tandem to develop knowledge of how technology can help students learn and understand subject matter.

The present case study uses the TPACK (Koehler and Mishra 2009) framework as well as the gradual release of responsibility model (Pearson and Gallagher 1983) to understand the attitudes, beliefs, knowledge and skills required for effective technology professional development and technology integration. A Canadian elementary school staff of teachers (Junior Kindergarten to Grade Eight) and their school principal engaged in professional learning to learn to use mobile multimedia technology (i.e. iPod Touch) as an instructional resource. The classroom-situated professional learning was facilitated by two university researchers from a teacher education department. The professional learning was organic in the sense that it evolved in response to the teachers' attitudes about using iPod Touches and their need for technological pedagogical content knowledge. The key role of the school principal is highlighted along with the facilitators' roles as coaches as the teachers began to gradually embrace the multimedia technology as an instructional resource.

The findings of this case study provide suggestions for designers of professional development programmes that aim to improve teachers' development of TPACK.

Teachers' attitudes on integrating technology in the classroom

Given the substantial expenditures on technology in schools, teachers and principals are under pressure to integrate these tools into classroom instruction in ways that are pedagogically sound (Swan and Dixon 2006). Because teachers and principals are the ultimate decision-makers on whether and how technology is used in the classroom, their attitudes and beliefs play a key role in implementation. Also, teachers' attitudes are a strong factor in determining technology usage (Bradshaw 2002), so it is important to ensure that technology training is compatible with their technology dispositions. Attitude in this study relates to several factors, including teachers' interest, comfort, confidence, apprehension and whether they feel the use of technology improves practice. In addition to teachers' attitudes, this study also considered the attitudes and actions of the school principal, because teachers are unlikely to embrace change without clear expectations and support from their principal (Hew and Brush 2007, McLeod and Richardson 2011).

In general, professionals tend to use or not use technology to the extent that they believe it will help them perform their tasks (perceived usefulness); even if they perceive technology as useful, they may still not use it if they believe the effort outweighs the benefits (Hixon and Buckenmeyer 2009). Teachers are no exception: teachers must be willing to accommodate new skills into their practice in order for change to occur. Such a commitment to continued professional learning is a basic underpinning of many professional standards associations. For example, the Ontario College of Teachers (2006) specifies that teachers, 'use appropriate resources and technology in planning for and responding to the needs of individual students and learning communities.'

Research on the elements of teachers' beliefs indicates that they are resistant to changing their practice and alter their views slowly (Vannatta and Fordham 2004). Why? The facilitation of teachers' professional growth (and change) is a complex process promoted by reflection, vicarious experiences, group and dyadic discussions, and the acquisition of new knowledge. There must be a commitment to use modified practices, accompanied by perceptions of increased student learning (Clarke and Hollingsworth 2002, Guskey 2002). Not surprisingly, teachers who do not feel comfortable with technology are less inclined to incorporate it into their plans (Jones 2001). Feelings of comfort and readiness to use technology come with time and instruction on how to use it (Swan and Dixon 2006). Increasing teachers' knowledge and skills related to how technology resources can help enhance their practice will improve their attitudes toward technology as attitudes and beliefs are a barrier to technology integration (Hew and Brush 2007). Consequently, teachers need time to engage in professional learning and training to become and remain proficient with technology integration (Luke *et al.* 1998, Bauer and Kenton 2005). Certainly the time investment is a worthwhile one, as professional learning that supports teachers' growth fosters educational improvement (Youngs 2001, Fullan *et al.* 2006). With the dynamic nature of technology, ongoing technology professional development must be valued and practised if teachers are to remain proficient.

Principal's support for technology and teachers' professional learning

Technology is best integrated into the curriculum when it is part of a school's goals, and accordingly the school principal plays a major role in this integration. School principals, similar to the UK head teacher, are charged with the leadership of teachers and the school community. Strong capacity-building leadership initiated by the school principal that includes securing resources and opportunities for teachers to collaborate during professional learning are key components of effective schools (Wolf *et al.* 2000). The principal's role as a technology leader includes developing and implementing professional growth plans and providing mentorship for teachers (Flanagan and Jacobsen 2003). The dedication is worth the investment as the technology leadership that a school principal provides can not only improve teachers' technological literacy but it directly encourages teachers to integrate technology into their instruction (Chang 2012). School principals' expectations and encouragement are vital for the infusion of technology into the educational process (Chin and Hortin 1994, Topp *et al.* 1995), especially when teachers are hesitant or resistant (Holland 2001).

One way principals can provide support is by providing teachers with release time for professional learning and training. According to a report on teacher use of technology (Smerdon *et al.* 2000), lack of release time to learn how to use technology for instruction was one of the greatest barriers to its use. Successful technology integration programmes provide: coaching, on-site services, just-in-time support that addresses teachers' needs, individualised instruction, observation of technology integration in practice and self-directed learning (Jacobsen 2001, 2002). Effective professional learning must provide opportunities for teachers to engage in discourse and reflection (Collet 2012). For decades it has been documented that such discussion among teachers about their practice can contribute to school improvement (for example, Richardson and Hamilton 1994, Rogoff *et al.* 1996, Taylor *et al.* 2005). Specifically, when teachers have the opportunity to engage in supported dialogue as they make connections to their students and classroom instruction, they often shift their beliefs and practice (Richardson and Hamilton 1994, Schnellert *et al.* 2008). Further, such collegial dialogue can engage teachers in critical reflection and goal-directed collaborations that enhance their knowledge and practice (Kelleher 2003, Butler *et al.* 2004). In particular, when collaborating with experienced colleagues, teachers who have immediate opportunities to apply new pedagogies and witness students' positive responses to changes in their instructional practice realise substantive changes in practice (Risko *et al.* 2009). In short, change is enabled when teachers and their experienced colleagues reflect on and dialogue together about instruction (Toll 2005).

In addition to the role of collegial discourse and practical application, professional learning should ideally be differentiated to complement teachers' prior experiences and knowledge (Hibbert *et al.* 2008, Kaasila and Lauriala 2010). Also, teacher professional learning should be responsive in terms of pace and content with respect to teachers' evolving learning needs (Crasborn 2008). This is especially the case with technology learning needs. These requirements of professional learning imply that the facilitators should understand teachers' readiness, customise the learning experiences to their learning profiles, provide opportunities for discussion and collaboration and support application in the classroom. For the current study, the facilitators/researchers adhered to these principles of optimal professional learning as they enabled a staff of elementary teachers to adopt a form of multimedia technology into their practice.

Theoretical framework

Typical approaches to technology-related professional development are based upon assumptions that it may be enough to just expose teachers to particular educational technologies (Harris *et al.* 2009). However, the competent twenty-first-century teacher no longer approaches teaching with technology using techno-centric strategies and techniques (teaching the tool); today, teachers require more than knowledge of technical skills in order to promote meaningful learning (Jonassen *et al.* 2008). Teaching technology skills (T in the TPACK model) in isolation does little to help teachers develop knowledge about: how to use technology to teach content in differentiated ways according to students' learning needs (TPK); how technology can be used to support the learning of specific curriculum content (TCK); or how to help students meet particular curriculum content standards while using technologies appropriately (TPACK) in their learning (Harris *et al.* 2009). Rather, teachers need to incorporate more content-centric approaches (teaching with the tool), addressing curricular topics in ways that are compatible with how their students learn (Harris *et al.* 2007, Jonassen *et al.* 2008). This can prove to be a daunting pursuit, one that has been described in the TPACK theoretical model (Mishra and Koehler 2006, Koehler and Mishra 2009).

As evident in this paper, the TPACK approach goes beyond techno-centric strategies and emphasises the importance of helping teachers develop and apply integrated and interdependent understandings of these three components of knowledge: technological, pedagogical and content knowledge (Koehler and Mishra 2009). TPACK depicts teacher knowledge and skills required for technology integration. According to Koehler and Mishra (2009), TPACK is a way of thinking strategically while involved in planning and organising for specific content, specific student needs and specific classroom situations while concurrently considering the multitude of twenty-first-century technologies with the potential for supporting student learning. TPACK-based professional development for teachers also needs to be flexible enough to accommodate the full range of teaching philosophies, styles, needs and approaches (Koehler and Mishra 2009). The TPACK approach holds that teachers' knowledge development is contextually situated and congruent with teachers' and students' learning needs and progress (Mishra and Koehler 2006, Koehler and Mishra 2009). That said, this paper provides insight into the development of the teacher participants' TPACK and learning trajectories, which were tailored to the specific academic contexts and needs of the teacher participants and their students.

Almost three decades ago, the gradual release of responsibility model (Pearson and Gallagher 1983) was introduced as one in which the educator scaffolds instruction for the learners. The educator mentors learners into becoming capable of handling tasks with which they have not yet developed expertise. Typically, the educator models metacognitive processes as an active learner and then provides guided instruction to facilitate learners through tasks that increase their understanding. Then learners collaborate to consolidate their understanding and begin to problem-solve and discuss with their peers. Such group and dyadic discussions have been well established within professional learning to support change in teachers' practice (Hixon and Buckenmeyer 2009). Finally, there is an opportunity for learners to engage in independent learning that includes practice in applying skills and learning to subsequent tasks to solidify their understanding. The gradual release of responsibility model is not linear as learners cycle through the components as they master skills and the educators provide suggestive and supportive feedback. This model was used as a framework for the facilitated programme of professional multimedia learning: the teacher participants were the learners and the professional learning facilitators/researchers were the educators.

Rationale for the study

For many schools, the focus has been on acquiring hardware and software rather than preparing teachers to use such technologies as a teaching tool and to integrate them across the curriculum (Sang *et al.* 2010). On average, school boards devote not more than 15% of technology budgets to teacher training (Sang *et al.* 2010). This was the situation for the school that is the focus of this case study. Funds had been spent on a class set of iPod Touches, yet professional learning and support had not been provided to the staff. Moreover, while numerous developers and industry sources are investing significant funds and intellectual resources toward developing app-based learning development efforts, there remains a dearth of information available to schools that is focused on mobile educational apps. Teachers need basic skills and confidence in using mobile multimedia technology, but they also need help integrating technology into their curriculum and instructional strategies.

This paper reports on the programme of professional learning in which a staff of elementary teachers (Junior Kindergarten to Grade Eight) and their principal from Ontario, Canada sought to learn to use a mobile multimedia device as an instructional resource. Accordingly, the following research questions were posed: What are the effects of the iPod Touch professional learning sessions on elementary teachers' and the principal's perceived self-efficacy and attitudes toward mobile multimedia technology use? How does the technology professional development and coaching influence teachers' professional learning? What is the principal's role in supporting use of the iPod Touch as an instructional resource for the classroom?

Methodology

This was a single-site case study undertaken to understand the impact of a technology professional learning programme on elementary teachers' attitudes towards mobile mulitimedia technology and their principal's role in the professional learning. Case studies are undertaken when educational researchers want to derive in-depth understandings of a particular phenomenon that is unique or unusual (Merriam 2001, Creswell *et al.* 2002, Yin 2003). In this sense, this single-case design was collective (Stake 1995) in that it tapped data from different sources, and it was descriptive (Yin 2003) in that it sought to describe the natural phenomena.

The role of the researchers was dual in the sense that they also facilitated the professional learning; however, the teachers dictated the direction and agenda of the programme. With this in mind, the potential for researchers' confirmation bias was minimised. The researchers are both experienced teacher educators with background in researching teachers' attitudes and beliefs about instructional practices and the integration of technology in education. Ethical procedures for conducting research with human participants were cleared by institutional research boards.

Professional learning sessions

In total, eight professional learning sessions were conducted over the course of four months by the two facilitators/researchers to familiarise the teachers with the iPod Touch, as well as to monitor teachers' progress of and discuss next steps for iPod Touch integration into their classroom instruction. Each teacher was also given a school-owned iPod Touch to use during the sessions and to use at their convenience between the sessions. The iPod Touch was not used for purposes other than education (for example, as a personal mobile device, wireless access at large). All of the teachers were provided with release time to attend the professional learning sessions. The facilitators prepared all of the iPod Touches (for example, application searching, downloading apps, synchronising iPods).

The first session (Introductory Phase) was held with all the teacher participants during a 50-minute class period. During this session, the facilitators introduced themselves to the group and outlined the rationale and objectives of the study. To familiarise them with the basic features and applications of the iPod Touch, the teachers and principal were given a glossary of iPod terms and apps and were led through a scavenger hunt activity to become familiar with using the iPod Touch.

In Session 2 (Planning Phase), the focus of the sessions moved to the pedagogical opportunities offered to teachers by the iPod Touch. Based on their selected curricular focus, the same-grade teachers collectively evaluated the quality and age-appropriateness of the downloaded iPod Touch applications for their classrooms. At the end of the meeting, the teachers were asked to complete a take-home exercise that required them to select one of the iPod applications they would like to subsequently use in a lesson.

In Sessions 3 and 6, each teacher participated in two separate co-planning sessions with one of the facilitators during school time. Using pre-selected iPod applications, the teacher and facilitator set lesson objectives, assessments and instructional activities, all of which correlated with Ontario's curriculum expectations. The various iPod Touch applications were used to learn, practice and explore concepts and skills from such curricular areas as literacy, mathematics, French, music, geography and history. The downloaded iPod apps were also facilitative of differentiated instruction because of the many setting features. Teachers could customise learning content to specific curricular and individual student needs, adjust the number of problems to present, as well as make progressive time adjustments (Banister 2010). These co-planning sessions were recorded through field notes. Then, approximately one week after each co-planning session with the individual teachers, the facilitators co-taught the iPod lessons (Sessions 4 and 7: Co-Teaching Phase).

During Sessions 5 and 8 (Post-Lesson Debriefing), the principal, teacher participants and facilitators reconvened to discuss the successes and struggles they encountered during the iPod lessons, as well as identify their next steps for integrating the iPod Touch into their classroom instruction. To forge home–school connections, the facilitators created a 'school–home–technology' section for the school website. Parents were provided with a list of iPod applications being used by their child and his/her classroom teacher, so that they were also able to support these applications at home.

School site and participants

The case was a staff within a Southern Ontario public elementary school in a small town. The school serves approximately 250 students (Junior Kindergarten to Grade Eight) in this mid-sized school board. It is important to note that every publicly funded school in Ontario, Canada is within a school board. Schools are grouped together into boards based on location, language and whether they are Catholic or non-denominational institutions. Each school board is responsible for the financial and organisational operations of its schools.

The female principal was also an integral member of the case, participating in all aspects of the professional learning and supporting the facilitators. She initiated the programme of professional learning described here. She is an experienced educator with former duties in the school board senior administration. She has been the principal for four years and at this school site for two years.

The case comprises 12 full-time elementary teachers (Junior Kindergarten to Grade Eight) and two half-time teachers – this is the entire school staff. They range in both teaching experience (i.e. less than one year to 30 years) and multimedia expertise (i.e. limited, some, lots). This profile information was gleaned from a survey that teachers completed. All teachers participated in the whole group sessions and were then given the option of whether to participate in co-planning and/or co-teaching sessions with the facilitators. There were eight teachers who participated in both the co-planning and co-teaching: Tamara, Melanie, Jodi, Martha, Brenda, Mario, Beth and Karl. The teachers that had previous experience with iPod Touches tended to be the ones who did not fully participate in the co-planning and/or co-teaching that was offered (e.g. John, Katie, Savanah, Penny, Priscilla, Lynn).

Data collection and analyses

There were three types of data collected from the teacher participants and the principal. At the beginning of the project a needs assessment was done, the Technology Experiences and Attitudes Teacher Questionnaire, and then the teachers and principal were interviewed to obtain their reflections on the professional learning experience. These data were coded independently by the two facilitators/researchers. The codes represented categories that were in response to the research questions. When the coding was complete, the two facilitators/researchers then came together to moderate the codes and regroup them into thematic clusters. The clusters were summarised and titled accordingly. Together, the facilitators/researchers selected data excerpts that most closely exemplified the themes and refined the theme titles. Following is a description of each type of data.

Technology Experiences and Attitudes Teacher Questionnaire

The Technology Experiences and Attitudes Teacher Questionnaire was administered to the participants prior to the professional learning sessions. This 25-item questionnaire was adapted from Lloyd and Gressard's (1984) Computer Attitude Scale (GLCAS) to suit the scope and local context of this study. For example, in adapting the GLCAS, the term 'computers' was replaced with 'mobile devices', and more specifically 'iPod Touch'. The GLCAS has been used in studies among pre-service teachers (Crowe and van't Hooft 2006) and in-service teachers (Lloyd and Gressard

1986, Christensen 2002). Lloyd and Gressard's (1986) reliability estimates for this scale ranged from 0.82 to 0.90 and a total score reliability of 0.95.

In this study, the Technology Experiences and Attitudes Teacher Questionnaire was used to measure the teacher participants' pre-training experiences with and attitudes toward technology in general and mobile devices such as the iPod Touch (technological knowledge). The questionnaire included three parts: background information (e.g. years of classroom experience, gender, teacher education level, certification status); technology professional development (e.g. amount and type of technology professional development and training); and technology experiences, beliefs and attitudes (e.g. technology proficiency, frequency of teacher and student use of technology in the classroom, attitudes toward technology and technology integration).

For the purposes of describing this case of 14 teachers and their principal, the following is a synopsis of the findings from the Technology Experiences and Attitudes Teacher Questionnaire. Regarding recent professional learning in technology, none of the teachers had taken any additional courses or participated in any peer networks or action-research-oriented groups devoted to technology in the classroom. Approximately one-half of the teachers had recently done some professional reading and engaged in informal peer dialogue on technology in education. Almost all of the teachers had recently attended school-board-facilitated workshops in either SMARTboard use and/or class website development. All of the teachers agreed with the potential of technology to enhance student learning and they believed that any necessary extra planning and preparation was justified. They all disagreed with the statement that they only use technology in the classroom when they are told to do so. The vast majority of the teacher participants stated that they did not hesitate to use technology as long as they look competent and they did not feel apprehensive about using an iPod Touch. Yet almost all teacher participants expressed the need for an experienced person to guide them in the use of an iPod Touch (for instructional purposes), while they did not see the need for an experienced person when using other types of technology.

An open-ended item was the final question on the Technology Experiences and Attitudes Teacher Questionnaire asking the teacher participants about their expectations of the upcoming iPod professional learning workshops. As evidenced in the following examples, their responses echoed both professional learning goals and student learning engagement:

I want to be able to use the iPods to enhance the children's learning. (Brenda)

My goal is to become confident and independent in using iPods and to be given some good ideas for using with kids. (Mario)

My main goal is to be better able to implement the iPod Touch in the class in order to increase student interest. (Beth)

The questionnaire was also used to identify the curriculum subject strand(s) that the teachers planned to teach with the iPods. This information was subsequently used by the facilitators to locate iPod applications (downloaded by the facilitators from the Apple App Store). In this way, the professional learning was highly responsive to the teachers' identified needs.

Teacher and principal interviews

At the end of the four months of professional learning, interviews were conducted with the teacher participants and the principal. The interview prompts were presented to determine whether a shift in teacher attitude and self-efficacy related to the iPod Touch occurred as a result of the technology professional learning. Questions also focused on the self-reported impact on professional learning and teaching, its influence on student learning, and pre-training and post-training changes in teachers' intentions toward technology integration. Ten of the teacher participants took part in this 30-minute, semi-structured individual interview. All interviews were audio-taped and transcribed by the two facilitators/researchers.

To gain the principal's perspective, one of the facilitators/researchers conducted a face-to-face, semi-structured interview with the school principal at the conclusion of the project. The purpose of this interview was to investigate the principal's perceptions of how the iPod professional learning sessions influenced student and teacher learning outcomes as well as impacted the self-efficacy of her teaching staff in using the iPod Touch in their classrooms. The 45-minute interview was audio-recorded and transcribed by one of the facilitators/researchers. All of the participants were provided with a copy of the interpretations of their insights for review, clarification, and verification of accuracy (that is, member checks).

Findings

The findings are presented in clusters that describe the teacher participants' initial attitudinal barriers including their technophobia (technological knowledge). As the teachers engaged in the professional learning, they commented on how this open-ended and responsive form of scaffolding offered them time to explore the technology and many supports along the way. Sustainability of the support is also addressed in the findings. The findings also highlight the elementary school principal's technology leadership role, which was strongly correlated with teachers' integration of the iPod Touch into the learning environment. The principal's leadership goals, competencies, responsibilities and strategies that were necessary for effective utilisation of the iPod Touch in schooling are described.

Attitudinal barriers and technophobia

In regard to teachers' technological knowledge (Koehler and Mishra 2009), the questionnaire findings outlined that the majority of the teachers at this school had little personal or professional experience using the iPod Touch. Personal familiarity builds confidence and assuages fears when implementing new methods or assimilating new knowledge. In some cases the teachers' fears had erected initial attitudinal barriers to using the class set of iPods and contributed to a form of technophobia:

> My comfort level is better than what it was ... when we first started it took me about 10 minutes to actually log on and it was frustrating; but now it takes much less time. So it's a matter of me playing with it as well, the more comfortable I am with it, the easier I am when I am working with the students. (Brenda, teacher, Grade Three)

The teachers noted that it was particularly advantageous to have time to become familiarised with the iPod Touch in a non-threatening environment. Providing the teachers with exposure and experience using the technology was a valuable investment in overcoming their attitudinal barriers. This takes time – time that needs to be built into the professional learning plan.

A few of the teachers internalised their lack of experience with the iPod Touch, citing their age and experience with other long-standing forms of technology. This disposition was one that echoed an internal locus of control, yet was somewhat uncontrollable as it was attributable to their prior experience and generation:

> I think that a barrier is me in terms of my physical dexterity. When you have big fingers it is difficult to use. I found it frustrating to type what I wanted to and I kept thinking that if I had a keyboard it would be zip … done! I guess this is a generational thing as young kids just have no problem. I kept wanting to pull it out and stretch it and make it bigger. (Mario, teacher, Grades Three/Four)

> There is a learning curve for all of this technology and it really takes time to sit down and spend time in front of it [iPod Touch]. It can become overwhelming at first when you have to learn along the way. … It takes me so long to learn. So that aspect for me personally is frustrating. But I say to myself, these are the things that I do well and these are the things that I have to do. (Karl, teacher, Grades Seven/Eight)

Embracing the iPod Touch technology was tempered with a dose of evaluation of the skills necessary to become adept at using it. This was only somewhat of an attitudinal barrier – more so, a caution prior to proceeding with implementation.

Supportive professional learning

As mentioned above, TPACK is a context-specific technological pedagogical and content knowledge (Koehler and Mishra 2009). Training teachers solely on how to use a specific technology is not likely to improve the practice of teaching and learning (Mishra and Koehler 2006). Teachers should be given ample opportunities to think through, critically choose or design and configure, learn and apply technologies that will best meet the teaching and learning needs that exist within their classroom and school context (Koehler and Mishra 2009). This specificity of context was portrayed in the teacher participants' interviews. The teacher participants reported that their professional learning needs were context specific when it came to enhancing their practice with the iPod Touch. They expressed their appreciation to have time to become familiar with the applications of the technology in a safe environment and without immediate implementation expectations. It was essential that these opportunities were relevant to their classroom assignments:

> For any technology workshop I find that if they are only explaining it, it isn't helpful. I went to one that had a PowerPoint presentation and you had the PowerPoint paper in front of you. But my hands were not on the keyboard. For me, I don't know whether it's that kinesthetic tactile learning, but I need to be able to like, 'Oh OK then I have to move this over here.' So if you don't have it in your hands, it doesn't make much sense … It's one thing to just sit, watch and listen. It is not until you can use it and manipulate it or else it doesn't stick. (Katie, teacher, Grades Three/Four)

Efficiency of transfer into their grade-specific curriculum was an important aspect of this professional learning. Another component was the immediacy and hands-on experience with the applications and the iPod Touch.

The teachers also appreciated the responsive nature of the professional learning. They too had learning needs that required differentiating as some teachers were less experienced with the iPod Touches than others. This was interpreted as the first step in the gradual release of responsibility for learning:

> I liked how the PD was hands-on and how we team-taught the first lesson because it helped to lower my initial 'how am I going to tackle this with 4 year olds?' ... hearing the language that you used with the children ('it just means that it's gone to sleep, push the button to wake it up') was helpful for me when I was modeling it with the other students to use that same language. (Tamara, teacher, Grades Junior Kindergarten/Senior Kindergarten)

> You found specific apps for what we were doing in the curriculum and also how we could get our own apps, and I could use them right away on the iPod. This is important for all in the school and to teach everyone in the school so they are all using them. You did everything for the gradual release of responsibility. You showed us and then you let us do it on our own and that was amazing. You differentiated because we didn't have to do it but you could sign up for help in your class if you needed it. It was really helpful for everybody. (Savanah, teacher, Grades Seven/Eight)

> You can download stuff online and read it or have a specialist come in but I need to actually see someone up there in action so then I know how to model it properly and comfortably. I don't have the time to read something on paper; I actually need to see it and be a part of it ... What was best for me was when you came into the classroom and we worked together [co-planning] and I could listen to the way you teach [modelling] it so I knew and I was comfortable when you left. (Martha, teacher, Grades One/Two)

The teachers expressed the effectiveness of engaging in their own hands-on learning with the co-planning, modelling, co-teaching and coaching support of the facilitators. Again, the relevance of the apps was important so that the teachers could see immediate applications into their curriculum.

The teachers acknowledged a common issue in using any new resource is the time needed to actually begin implementation. With the business of the regular school day and many time constraints, it is sometimes difficult to take the figurative 'shrink wrap' off the new resource and actually crack it open. The facilitators did this step and the teachers commented about this aspect of the professional learning experience:

> All of the different apps that have been added and sorted have been a HUGE [help to me]. This has been helpful. Downloading apps is so time consuming. I was doing this at home and I had all of these weird apps on my iPod. A lot of them we couldn't buy so I was only getting the free apps so now that it is all set up with the educational apps. This is something that I could not have done, so it is so helpful. A lot of the time I would not have been able to find those apps. I don't know how you found those apps. (Savanah, teacher, Grades Seven/Eight)

Key to the perceived effectiveness of the professional learning was the preparation that the facilitators devoted to readying the iPods. This is similar to doing background research and preparing student resources prior to a lesson. This step afforded the teachers the opportunity to simply think about implementation in the classroom.

Typically with any form of professional learning, there is the question of long-term sustainability and impact on future practice. The teacher participants and principal expressed their thoughts on this and offered follow-up suggestions:

> I think that as with any initiative, the cycling back is so important. So next year, even though we don't have the iPod project, we have to keep cycling back and asking the teachers, 'How are you using it? How is it helping you achieve your goal? Let's make sure it is still part of our action plan to use them.' (Lindsay, principal)

The teachers and their principal realistically acknowledged that sustainability in the professional learning is their responsibility. They did express the value in the facilitators following up with them as a form of accountability.

Principal as technology leader

In addition to diverse expectations and responsibilities, contemporary school principals are also being called upon to be leaders of technological change. The special challenge for the principal is being a technology leader as well as encouraging the development of teacher and student technology leaders. This theme highlights the key role that the school principal played not only in supporting technology, but also in facilitating change and developing strategies to increase technology utilisation among the classroom teachers, especially those who were hesitant to embrace technology.

Teacher reluctance was one of the challenges cited by the principal as affecting the implementation of technology. The principal referred to the conscious competence model (Charlton 2001) to explain the varying levels of technological competence among her teaching staff:

> Bringing Savanah [Grades Seven/Eight teacher] in who is very technology savvy and willing to share helps as well because she's doing all these things with the students and the teachers are seeing that. (Lindsay, principal)

> I think that there are four types of stages of learning that you go through. The first stage is unconscious incompetence – 'I have no idea what I don't know', conscious incompetence – 'I know that I don't know that' ... we had some teachers who were consciously aware and reluctant at first and said to me 'I'm just afraid, I don't know how to do it!' The third stage is conscious competence, and the fourth is unconscious competence – those who are unconsciously able to use technology, and they haven't quite realized that they are really good. Sometimes we think we are consciously competent and great at something and so we don't open ourselves up to it. We had a couple of people on staff who said 'Oh I'm so good at this, I don't need this', but everybody needs it. (Lindsay, principal)

Lindsay was aware of the attitudes of her teachers toward integrating new technology. This awareness was the key to highlighting how technology was a part of the school's improvement plan and an instrumental means for providing students with another learning device:

> All of the teachers had to make the same 'if ... then' goal. We made the technology – not the goal – but the technology was the action plan to get there. On our action plan, it was, 'How can we use the iPods to help me get to the goal?' My teachers really seem to understand that it's one of the effective instructional practices ... it's another

avenue to reach these kids, and it's an avenue that these kids really, really like. So when we schedule iPod or computer time, it's not because we want iPods, it is because it's helping us get to where we need to get to. (Lindsay, principal)

We had a check-up sheet, and everybody had to do a self-reflection. I asked them, 'Where are you with our iPod Project?' Then we shared, and everyone was put on the spotlight, and a few staff members went, 'Oh my goodness, I haven't done any of these things!' And I could quite calmly say, 'The expectation is that you participate in these projects – these are not the common goal – these are the ways you are going to get to your goal.' So at the staff meeting it was very clear that the expectation was they take part in some of these projects. (Lindsay, principal)

The overriding message that can also be gleaned from the principal's words is that the technology is a means, not an end. That is, the iPod is a tool for achieving instructional goals, not a goal in itself. The principal emphasised that before schools invest in any technology equipment, they need to set goals and articulate a vision for iPod integration that is shared, understood and acted upon by all.

After the educational goals and vision of learning through technology have been determined, the principal believed that teachers need to be provided with professional learning in order to help them choose the most appropriate technologies and instructional strategies to meet the school's goals. The principal described the steps and strategies utilised for translating her school technology vision into reality and facilitating the teachers' integration of the iPod Touch into their curricula. The principal noted that an appropriate balance of pressure, time, collaboration, support and resources for professional learning is needed to effectively facilitate technological change:

You really need to give teachers the PD, the time, resources, materials, make them participants and give them choice to be able to achieve their goals. It's one thing giving them the technology equipment and saying, 'OK here you go!' but you also have to go in there and say, 'Can I get you some resources?' and give them lots of support and opportunity to talk together – whether it's in PLCs or in shared planning time – about those kinds of things. Last year was a perfect example, because they had an iPod lab in the school and it was not used until we gave them the PD and coaching this year. (Lindsay, principal)

In applying pressure to continue to grow professionally, the principal made the teachers responsible for their own means of achieving their goals. She recognised that her role was to mobilise the necessary supports such as coaching, and to guide from the side as they collaborated and all learned together.

Discussion

The first research question sought to describe the teachers' initial and post-professional learning attitudes and self-efficacy toward mobile multimedia technology use. An initial lack of knowledge and confidence was apparent in the majority of the staff who had put forth attitudinal barriers to using the iPod Touches. Additionally, uncontrollable reasons for not having prior experience with the technology were cited. The teacher participants remarked that the time provided to simply 'play' with the iPods was helpful and some stated that they might proceed with caution until the full educational value of the device is apparent. These apprehensions have been expressed in other studies (for example, Hixon and Buckenmeyer 2009) that identify teachers' core values about teaching as the significant obstacles to overcome toward technology integration in the classroom. Hixon and Buckenmeyer (2009) assert that for technology professional learning to be successful, it must be individualised and not offered in plenary group training sessions.

The teachers' impressions of the technology professional development and coaching were the focus of the second research question. One of the findings specifically highlighted the fact that the teachers acknowledged the responsive nature of the professional learning. The teachers had learning needs that required differentiating as some were less experienced with the iPod Touches than others. These needs were addressed in the programme of professional learning that was facilitated. This was interpreted as the first step in the gradual release of responsibility for learning. The pacing of the professional learning was an important feature to minimise overwhelm and assimilate the technology into the teachers' personal and professional skill set. They also appreciated the preparation time that facilitators invested to ready the devices with apps that were grade appropriate and curricular timely. Ongoing support through co-planning, co-teaching and coaching contributed to the gradual release of responsibility for learning (Pearson and Gallagher 1983) that the teachers experienced. Evidence of the initial effectiveness of the professional learning can be inferred from the teachers' and principal's expressions of the desire for follow up to the professional learning.

In answer to the second research question, the TPACK (Mishra and Koehler 2006, Koehler and Mishra 2009) framework laid a powerful foundation for the teacher participants in the present study. This programme provided situated, hands-on learning opportunities for participating teachers to build and sustain communities of practice, which seemed to have positive impacts on their technology integration. Each teacher was also given a school-owned iPod Touch to use during the subsequent professional learning sessions, which afforded teachers the opportunity to learn to simultaneously blend technology use with content and pedagogical strategies (Mishra and Koehler 2006). Moreover, by providing a forum for their collaboration, participants were able to discuss technical and curriculum questions, classroom management issues and assessment practices. The teachers discussed how to use the iPod technology, and shared tips and short cuts they learned while using the technology tools in their respective classrooms.

One of the other features of the professional learning to which the teachers also responded favourably was the co-planning and co-teaching with the facilitators. Continuous and individualised support also helped the teachers overcome the constraints and concerns in incorporating technology so that they felt efficacious in teaching their curricular content using technology (Koehler and Mishra 2009). The collaboration within the context of the professional learning sessions was the part that made the technophobic teachers more confident and comfortable to teach with the iPod technology. The teachers valued working with the facilitators; the collaboration during the one-on-one planning sessions helped foster growth in teachers' technological pedagogical content knowledge and skills, which in turn led to an increase in the teachers' perceptions of computer self-efficacy (Koehler and Mishra 2009). Planning with their grade-specific curriculum outcomes in mind, having the facilitators model activities with the iPod Touch and co-teaching lessons are all aspects that contribute to teachers' enhanced practice with technology (Figg and Jaipal-Jamani 2009, 2011). These are technology pedagogical skills that are essential for teaching with technology (Figg and Jaipal-Jamani 2009, 2011) and the teachers received some of these through this professional learning experience. This reality addresses the need for professional learning facilitators to not lose sight of how to enhance teacher knowledge for technology integration into instruction.

With respect to the teachers' perceptions of the students' learning, we also found that the use of the iPod Touch appeared to have catapulted students into the role of 'teacher' and teachers into the role of 'learner' in immediate and obvious ways (Ciampa and Gallagher under review). The students' own perceptions of their social experience took on a new dimension when they were the technology experts in the classroom, and some of their teachers were positioned in a novice role. These findings highlight the shifting dynamics in a technology-enriched classroom where such practices as (cross-age) peer mentoring and reciprocal teaching are fostered. The iPod Touch also provided affordances for supporting instructional activities in K–8 education that enabled differentiated instruction by the teacher and personalised learner-centric educational experiences by the students (Ciampa and Gallagher under review). In this case, the teachers played a minimal role in helping individual learners take control of the learning process. Individual learners decided where and when to learn and personalised their learning environments.

We also garnered parents' perceptions of their children's use of iPods for classroom instruction (Ciampa and Gallagher under review). Similar to the teachers' responses, one of the most obvious positive student outcomes that parents reported was enhanced student engagement. Likewise, parents also agreed that their digitally experienced children are self-directed, autonomous learners when they use the iPod Touch. This was reflective of the students' increased familiarity and proficiency with the mobile tool.

The final research question aimed at profiling the principal's role in supporting the use of the iPod Touch as an instructional resource for classroom use. In this case study, the principal was a technology leader who had developed and implemented a vision and technology plan for her school, and this is an integral factor contributing to teachers' technological literacy (Chang 2012). The principal sought to create change in teaching practices and support the technology learning needs of her staff. She acknowledged the fact that the teachers were on different levels of technological competence and acceptance, and therefore required differentiated types of professional learning experiences, support and collaboration. The principal's goal for technology implementation was grounded in enhancing the instructional process and providing students with another learning tool. The role of the principal in this case study was integral to its success as this principal supported the gradual release of responsibility for the teachers' professional learning (Frey and Fisher 2009). Similar to enhanced student learning when teachers release responsibility for their learning, when the principal supports professional learning that gradually releases responsibility for teachers' learning, their learning is maximised.

The technology professional learning programme described herein yielded outcomes that are verified in pre-existing literature. According to Flanagan and Jacobsen (2003), effective technology professional learning requires support for ongoing, timely sessions that focus on experimentation and collaboration among teachers. Fullan (2001a) also characterised collaborative culture as critical in successful schools, where risk-taking and idea-sharing are fundamental to improving the quality of instruction and learning. These approaches are grounded in the interactions between and among learning community members. When interactions are reciprocal, individuals contribute mutually to a shared vision and engender mutual benefits that encourage a 'culture of collaboration among teachers' (Glazer *et al.* 2009, p. 29). This qualitative study allows for a deeper understanding of how the technology professional learning sessions impacted teachers' self-efficacy beliefs, attitudes and practice and the role that their principal played in this.

Conclusions and implications

In evaluating the professional learning facilitation process herein, several factors contributed to its relative success while modifications could have also contributed to enhanced outcomes. At the most basic level, the gradual release of responsibility modelled by the facilitators respected the teachers' varied zones of proximal development (with respect to their knowledge and experience with iPods) and supported their increasing competencies (Collet 2012). Further, collaboration among educators (both facilitators and participants) was an essential factor that promoted teacher change and improved educational outcomes (Fullan 2001b). These were the positive outcomes of the project, but are they realistic? Dedicated and knowledgeable facilitators such as those who led this study are not always available and school boards may not have the resources to devote personnel to such professional learning projects. In addition, it is not often the case that a school possesses a class set of mobile technologies such as the iPod Touch. This provision made it easy for the teachers to access the resources that they needed so that they might begin to implement them into their classrooms.

Future directions to enhance teacher professional learning in technology need to include supports for teachers' engagement in critical reflection on information (Clarke and Hollingsworth 2002). Reflective practice can also help teachers improve their knowledge of pedagogy and knowledge of students (Shoffner 2009). Facilitators of technology professional learning need to know how to engage teachers in the type of robust reflection that is required for change, as well as provide teachers with opportunities to share their experiences with their peers. This critical reflection is requisite to foster conceptual awareness, which is a necessary initial step in supporting change in teachers' practices (Gregoire 2003, Loughran 2007). Teachers need to be able to acknowledge their current practices, be open to alternative practices and then identify the efficacy of new practices (Cochran-Smith and Lytle 2009). Importantly, the critical reflection required for teachers to entertain changes to their beliefs and practices should be initiated through non-threatening reflective dialogue such as the dialogue that was a part of the process in this project (Duffy 2005).

This type of case-study work could be executed in subsequent studies and in multiple sites provided there are research funds, supportive facilitators and a principal who supports the use of technology in education. Future research might investigate the contributions of teacher technology leaders (within the school site) to support such professional learning projects. Finally, a valuable contribution to the literature would be a study of the impact of teacher professional learning in technology on the learning and motivation of students.

A final thought that both the teacher participants and their principal offered was to consider how to follow-up and sustain the professional learning. It is often the case that, left unattended, professional learning goes unreinforced. Glazer *et al.*

(2009) provided elementary teachers with technology professional learning through a collaborative, peer-mentoring programme. Factors that contributed to this programme's success included guidance from a knowledgeable peer, co-planning and modelling, but also building sustainable relationships such as expert–novice dyads and proximity within the same school. To continue the collaborative professional learning, Glazer *et al.* (2009) recommend that the working relationships remain responsive and flexible and seek to find curricular area similarities.

Engagement is the key to student learning but it is also integral to teacher professional learning. Participating in technology professional learning that is relevant and differentiated for teachers includes planning and developing lessons that address their grade-level curriculum while incorporating mobile technology such as the iPod Touch. There is a need for teachers to become proficient designers of instruction with these tools. We have described a programme of professional learning to highlight aspects of teachers' attitudinal dispositions and the role of the principal as technology leader that contribute to successful design of technologically enhanced teaching and learning experiences in a classroom.

References

Banister, S., 2010. Integrating the iPod touch in K–12 education: visions and vices. *Computers in the schools*, 27 (2), 121–131. doi: 10.1080/07380561003801590.

Bauer, J. and Kenton, J., 2005. Toward technology integration in the schools: why it isn't happening. *Journal of technology and teacher education*, 13 (4), 519–546.

Bradshaw, L., 2002. Technology for teaching and learning: strategies for staff development and follow-up support. *Journal of technology and teacher education*, 10 (1), 131–150.

Butler, D.L., *et al.*, 2004. Collaboration and self-regulation in teachers' professional development. *Teaching and teacher education*, 20 (5), 435–455.

Carlson, S. and Gadio, C.T., 2002. Teacher professional development in the use of technology. *In*: W.D. Haddad and A. Draxler, eds. *Technologies for education: potential, parameters, and prospects*. Paris and Washington, DC: UNESCO and AED, 118–132.

Chang, I., 2012. The effect of principals' technological leadership on teachers' technological literacy and teaching effectiveness in Taiwanese elementary schools. *Journal of educational technology and society*, 15 (2), 328–340.

Charlton, G., 2001. *Human habits of highly effective organizations*. Pretoria: Van Schaik.

Chin, S. and Hortin, J.A., 1994. Teachers' perceptions of instructional technology and staff development. *Journal of educational technology systems*, 22 (2), 83–98.

Christensen, R., 2002. Effects of technology integration education on the attitudes of teachers and students. *Journal of research on technology in education*, 34 (4), 411–433.

Ciampa, K. and Gallagher, T.L., under review. Getting in touch: facilitating the use of the iPod Touch in the elementary classroom. *Computers & education*.

Clarke, D. and Hollingsworth, H., 2002. Elaborating a model of teacher professional growth. *Teaching and teacher education*, 18 (8), 947–967.

Cochran-Smith, M. and Lytle, S.L., 2009. *Inquiry as stance: practitioner research for the next generation*. New York, NY: Teachers College Press.

Collet, V., 2012. The gradual increase of responsibility model: coaching for teacher change. *Literacy research and instruction*, 51 (1), 27–47.

Crasborn, F., 2008. Promoting versatility in mentor teachers' use of supervisory skills. *Teaching and teacher education*, 24 (3), 499–514.

Creswell, J.W., *et al.*, 2002. *Educational research: planning, conducting, and evaluating quantitative and qualitative research*. Upper Saddle River, NJ: Merrill Prentice Hall.

Crowe, A. and van't Hooft, M.A.H., 2006. Technology and the prospective teacher: using handheld devices in social studies education. *Current issues in technology and teacher education*, 6 (1), 99–119.

Druin, A., 2009. Introduction: mobile technologies, children, and learning. *In*: A. Druin, ed. *Mobile technology for children: designing for interaction and learning*. San Francisco, CA: Morgan Kaufmann, 17–21, –.

Duffy, G.G., 2005. Developing metacognitive teachers: visioning and the expert's changing role in teacher education and professional development. *In*: S.E. Israel, *et al.*, eds. *Metacognition in literacy learning*. Mahwah, NJ: Lawrence Erlbaum, 299–314, –.

Figg, C. and Jaipal Jamani, K., 2009. Engaging 21st century learners and differentiating instruction with technology. *Teaching and learning*, 5 (1), 1–12.

Figg, C. and Jaipal Jamani, K., 2011. Exploring teacher knowledge and actions supporting technology-enhanced teaching in elementary schools: two approaches by pre-service teachers. *Australasian journal of educational technology*, 27 (7), 1227–1246.

Flanagan, L. and Jacobsen, D.M., 2003. Technology leadership for the 21st century principal. *Journal of educational administration*, 41 (2), 124–142.

Frey, N. and Fisher, D., 2009. The release of learning. *Principal leadership*, 9 (6), 18–22.

Fullan, M., 2001a. *Leading in a culture of change*. San Francisco, CA: Jossey-Bass.

Fullan, M., 2001b. *The new meaning of educational change*. New York, NY: Teachers College Press.

Fullan, M., Hill, P., and Crevola, C., 2006. *Breakthrough*. Thousand Oaks, CA: Corwin Press.

Glazer, E., *et al.*, 2009. Factors and interactions influencing technology integration during situated professional development in an elementary school. *Computers in the schools*, 26 (1), 21–39.

Gregoire, M., 2003. Is it a challenge or a threat? A dual-process model of teachers' cognition and appraisal during conceptual change. *Educational psychology review*, 15 (2), 147–179.

Guskey, T.R., 2002. Professional development and teacher change. *Teachers and teaching: theory and practice*, 8 (3/4), 381–391.

Harris, J.B., Mishra, P., and Koehler, M.J., 2007. Teachers' technological pedagogical content knowledge: curriculum-based technology integration reframed. *Paper presented at the 2007 Annual Meeting of the American Educational Research Association (AERA)*, 10 April, Chicago, IL.

Harris, J., Mishra, P., and Koehler, M.J., 2009. Teachers' technological pedagogical content knowledge and learning activity types: curriculum-based technology integration reframed. *Journal of research on technology in education*, 41 (4), 393–416.

Hew, K.F. and Brush, T., 2007. Integrating technology into K–12 teaching and learning: current knowledge gaps and recommendations for future research. *Educational technology research and development*, 55 (3), 223–252.

Hibbert, K.M., Heydon, R.M., and Rich, S.J., 2008. Beacons of light, rays, or sun catchers? A case study of the positioning of literacy teachers and their knowledge in neoliberal times. *Teaching and teacher education*, 24 (2), 303–315.

Hixon, E. and Buckenmeyer, J., 2009. Revisiting technology integration in schools: implications for professional development. *Computers in the schools*, 26 (2), 130–146.

Holland, P.E., 2001. Professional development in technology: catalyst for school reform. *Journal of technology and teacher education*, 9 (2), 245–267.

Jacobsen, D.M., 2001. Building different bridges: technology integration, engaged student learning, and new approaches to professional development. *Paper presented at the 82nd Annual Meeting of the American Educational Research Association*, 10 April, Seattle, WA.

Jacobsen, D.M., 2002. Building different bridges two: a case study of transformative professional development for student learning with technology. *Paper presented at the 83rd Annual Meeting of the American Educational Research Association*, 1 April, New Orleans, LA.

Jonassen, D., *et al.*, 2008. *Meaningful learning with technology*. 3rd ed. Upper Saddle River, NJ: Pearson.

Jones, C., 2001. Tech support: preparing teachers to use technology. *Principal leadership*, 1 (9), 35–39.

Kaasila, R. and Lauriala, A., 2010. Towards a collaborative, interactionist model of teacher change. *Teaching and teacher education*, 26 (4), 854–862.

Kelleher, J., 2003. A model for assessment driven professional development. *Phi delta kappan*, 84 (10), 751–756.

Koehler, M.J. and Mishra, P., 2009. What is technological pedagogical content knowledge? *Contemporary issues in technology and teacher education*, 9 (1) [online]. Available from: http://www.citejournal.org/vol9/iss1/general/article1.cfm [Accessed 20 July 2012].

Lawless, K.A. and Pellegrino, K.W., 2007. Professional development in integrating technology into teaching and learning: knowns, unknowns, and ways to pursue better questions and answers. *Review of educational research*, 77 (4), 575–614.

Loughran, J., 2007. Enacting a pedagogy of teacher education. *In*: T. Russell and J. Loughran, eds. *Enacting a pedagogy of teacher education: values, relationships and practices*. New York, NY: Routledge, 1–15, –.

Loyd, B.H. and Gressard, C., 1984. Reliability and factoral validity of computer attitude scale. *Educational and psychological measurement*, 44 (2), 501–505.

Loyd, B.H. and Gressard, C., 1986. The reliability and validity of an instrument for the assessment of computer attitudes. *Educational and psychological measurement*, 45 (4), 903–908.

Luke, N., *et al.*, 1998. Authentic approaches to encourage technology-using teachers. *Paper presented at the Society for Information Technology and Teacher Education international conference*, 10 March, Washington, DC.

McLeod, S. and Richardson, J.W., 2011. The dearth of technology coverage. *Journal of school leadership*, 21 (2), 216–240.

Merriam, S.B., 2001. *Qualitative research and case study applications in education. Revised and expanded from case study research in education*. 2nd ed. San Francisco, CA: Jossey-Bass.

Ministry of Education of Ontario, 2007. *The Ontario curriculum grades 1–8*. Toronto, ON: Author.

Mishra, P. and Koehler, M.J., 2006. Technological pedagogical content knowledge: a new framework for teacher knowledge. *Teachers college record*, 108 (6), 1017–1054.

Ontario College of Teachers, 2006. *The standards of practice for the teaching profession* [online]. Available from: http://www.oct.ca/standards/standards_of_practice.aspx?lang=en-CA [Accessed 23 July 2012].

Pearson, P.D. and Gallagher, M.C., 1983. The instruction of reading comprehension. *Contemporary educational psychology*, 8 (3), 317–344.

Richardson, V. and Hamilton, M.L., 1994. The practical argument staff development process. *In*: V. Richardson, ed. *Teacher change and the staff development process: a case of reading instruction*. New York, NY: Teachers College Press, 109–134, –.

Risko, V.J., *et al.*, 2009. Making sense of reading teacher education research and prospects for future research. *Paper presented at the annual conference of the International Reading Association*, 3 May, Minneapolis, MN.

Rogoff, B., Matusov, B., and White, S., 1996. Models of teaching and learning: participation in a community of learners. *In*: D. Olson and N. Torrance, eds. *The handbook of cognition and human development*. Oxford: Blackwell, 388–414, –.

Sandholtz, J.H., 2001. Learning to teach with technology: a comparison of teacher development programs. *Journal of technology and teacher education*, 9 (3), 349–374.

Sang, G., *et al.*, 2010. Student teachers' thinking processes and ICT integration: predictors of prospective teaching behaviours with educational technology. *Computers & education*, 54 (1), 103–112.

Schnellert, L.M., Butler, D.L., and Higginson, S.K., 2008. Co-constructors of data, co-constructors of meaning: teacher professional development in an age of accountability. *Teaching and teacher education*, 24 (3), 725–750.

Shoffner, M., 2009. 'Because I know how to use it': integrating technology into preservice English teacher reflective practice. *Contemporary issues in technology and teacher education*, 9 (4), 371–391.

Smerdon, B., *et al.*, 2000. *Teachers' tools for the 21st century: a report on teachers' use of technology*. Washington, DC: US Department of Education, National Center for Education Statistics.

Stake, R.E., 1995. *The art of case study research*. London: Sage.

Swan, B. and Dixon, J., 2006. The effects of mentor-supported technology professional development on middle school mathematics teachers' attitudes and practice. *Contemporary issues in technology and teacher education*, 6 (1), 67–86.

Taylor, B.M., *et al.*, 2005. The CIERA School Change Project: an evidence-based approach to professional development and school reading improvement. *Reading research quarterly*, 40 (1), 40–69.

Toll, C.A., 2005. *The literacy coaches survival guide*. Newark, DE: International Reading Association.

Topp, N., Mortensen, R., and Grandgenett, N., 1995. Building a technology-using faculty to facilitate technology-using teachers. *Journal of computing in teacher education*, 11 (3), 11–14.

Vannatta, R.A. and Fordham, N., 2004. Teacher dispositions as predictors of classroom technology use. *Journal of research technology in education*, 36 (3), 253–272.

Wolf, S.A., *et al.*, 2000. 'That dog won't hunt!' Exemplary school change efforts within the Kentucky reform. *American educational research journal*, 37 (2), 349–393.

Yin, R.K., 2003. *Case study research: design and methods*. 3rd ed. Thousand Oaks, CA: Sage.

Youngs, P., 2001. District and state policy influences on professional development and school capacity. *Educational policy*, 15 (2), 278–301.

Research capacity-building with new technologies within new communities of practice: reflections on the first year of the Teacher Education Research Network

Zoe Fowler[a], Grant Stanley[b], Jean Murray[c], Marion Jones[b] and Olwen McNamara[d]

[a]Education Research Consultant, Cambridge, USA; [b]Faculty of Education, Community and Leisure, Liverpool John Moores University, Aigburth, Liverpool, UK; [c]Cass School of Education, University of East London, London, UK; [d]School of Education, The University of Manchester, Manchester, UK

This article focuses on a virtual research environment (VRE) and how it facilitated the networking of teacher educators participating in an Economic and Social Research Council-funded research capacity-building project. Using the theoretical lenses of situated learning and socio-cultural approaches to literacy, participants' ways of engaging with this technology are described, and the reasons why their existing technical expertise did not unproblematically transfer to the new technology are explored. We argue that three main factors affected the use of the VRE, and in particular its wiki tool: the individual's motivation to learn and to engage with (more) new technologies; the emerging dynamics of each research group as they developed shared working practices; and the institutional climates, which supported or discouraged the individuals' engagement with both the technology and a regional Teacher Education Research Network that used this technology. In conclusion, we suggest that successful engagement with new technologies in future academic communities of practice might well benefit from a shared commitment to agreed working practices across the group and the provision of brokerage and championing of the technology by key individuals who are in the position to inspire, motivate and support others.

Introduction

New technologies afford new ways of learning within the academy (Carmichael and Burchmore 2010, Conole and Alevizou 2010). Much has been discussed in relation to the changing academic literacies of students through emerging technologies (see, for example, Lea 2004, Goodfellow and Lea 2007, Ross 2011), but there is far less research on how such technologies might be deployed in the learning of academics themselves. This paper makes a contribution to addressing this deficiency by focusing upon the experiences and practices of a group of academics engaging with a new virtual research environment (VRE) for professional development purposes.

The Teacher Education Research Network (TERN) comprised academics working in the Schools of Education in seven higher education institutions across the North West of England. It was a capacity-building project, the primary purpose of which was to provide situated learning opportunities for 'early career researchers' wanting to develop their knowledge and understanding of research in education. Our focus in this paper is to explore how new technologies, namely the provision of the VRE, supported the collaborative, communicative, and mentoring practices of this network. Overall, the TERN project achieved high degrees of success and was judged by the external evaluator to have created, 'an active community of researchers successfully practising the principles of supportive interaction, collaboration and participation in the shared enterprise of building research-capacity' (Gardner 2009, p. 16). However, the uptake of the VRE was disappointing[1] and all TERN research groups eventually decided to move away from the VRE, instead using more familiar tools to mediate their collaborative work and not employing the VRE's wiki tool in drafting the research bids on which each group worked.

Using the theoretical lenses of situated learning (Lave and Wenger 1991, Eraut 2000, Evans *et al.* 2006) and socio-cultural approaches to literacy (Gee 1996, Street 2005), this paper considers the reasons for the less than straight-forward transfer of participants' existing expertise and level of engagement with other technology(ies) to usage of the VRE. Drawing on those frameworks and a large database of evidence, we discuss and analyse the complex causes of the limited uptake of the technology. We argue that the level/depth of engagement with the VRE was related to three factors: the individual's motivation to learn and to engage with (more) new technologies; the emerging dynamics of individual research groups as they developed shared working practices; and the institutional climates, which supported or discouraged the individuals' engagement with both the technology and the TERN project more widely (see also Murray *et al.* 2012). In the conclusion to the paper, we draw on our analyses to identify factors that we feel would facilitate successful engagement with new technologies in new communities of practice.

The Teacher Education Research Network

The TERN project began life in 2008, funded by the UK Economic and Social Research Council (ESRC) for one year as a pilot research capacity-building project. Its primary aim was to grow a regional research network in teacher education through developing an inter-institutional collaborative network of research groups. Previous analyses had confirmed the significant need for regional research capacity-building in teacher education, and the potential to enhance institutional research capacity through a project of this kind. Forty-four individuals were selected by their higher education institutions to participate in the network as research fellows, and the TERN management group allocated these participants on the basis of their expressed research interests to specific research groups. Each group also included one senior academic, a professor or a reader, who operated as a research mentor. The research groups provided situated learning environments where group members worked collaboratively, with the guidance and support of the mentor, to develop a communal research bid. This model of professional learning was informed by an embedded social practices approach to building research capacity (Baron 2005), which is underpinned by the principles of situated cognition and stresses the importance of informal professional learning through researchers engaging collaboratively in aspects of the research process (Rees *et al.* 2007). Network-wide events took place across the year, including formal presentations from leading academics in teacher education and educational research, and workshops tailored to the needs of participants who were at different stages within their professional careers (see Murray *et al.* 2011). The role of the technology was intended to support all of the situated learning within the project, but with particular emphasis on facilitating the development of the groups' research bids.

Each of the research groups was provided with an online worksite within the VRE that contained: an announcements tool, a data repository, both synchronous and asynchronous communication tools (i.e. [discussion] forums and chat room), and a collaborative 'wiki' that could be used for information management or for collaborative writing purposes (see Figure 1).

The software was developed by the Centre for Applied Research in Educational Technology (CARET) at the University of Cambridge as part of the ESRC's Teaching and Learning Research Programme (TLRP) and, prior to TERN, several of TLRP's research projects had used the VRE to support collaborative working practices and/or communication across research teams (Laterza *et al.* 2007). This technology was also formative to the development of communities of enquiry in the Applied Educational Research Scheme (AERS) (Wilson *et al.* 2007). During the first year of TERN, a sister ESRC-funded project, 'A Social and Professional Network for Early Career Researchers in Education', explored opportunities to develop more interactive features using this software to support the building of

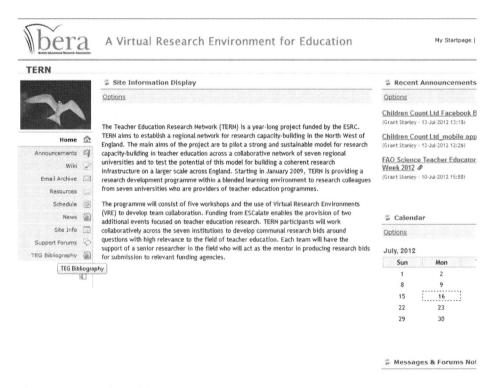

Figure 1.   Screenshot of the VRE interface showing the tools available in the left-hand menu.

research capacity in educational research (Carmichael 2009). TERN, therefore, was aiming to make use of a technology that had an established track record for supporting collaboration and communication within educational research groups and which presented potential affordances to support online mentoring, professional development opportunities, and collaborative activities. The initial time-frame for the project was 12 months, which was inevitably going to be a challenge, so the management group front-loaded scheduled VRE training sessions over the first three months of the project. It was anticipated that research groups would establish their own online working practices as they collaboratively developed their research bids: the utilisation of tools would be dependent upon the group's working practices rather than imposed through the TERN management group. This approach was informed by evidence showing that the worksites and their tools could be tailored to the needs and preferred practices of research groups (Carmichael *et al.* 2006, Wilson *et al.* 2007).

The data in this paper draw on the extensive project database, which included an initial questionnaire distributed to all participants at the start of the pilot year; an exit questionnaire, which gathered reflective data on participation, learning within the groups, and evaluations of the technology; exit interviews with a sample of research fellows and research mentors; and field notes from the VRE coaching sessions. Additionally, this paper utilises data from a textual analysis of each group's VRE activities. These data were preserved within the VRE during the pilot year, and analysed using basic statistics and a coding approach drawn from grounded theory. Full details of all aspects of the research design and a more detailed description of analysis are available in Murray *et al.* (2011) and Gardner (2009). Here we focus, in particular, on the patterns shown through analysis of three of the groups' online engagements in the VRE.

The TERN project rested upon clear, rigorous and detailed ethical principles, based on the guidance provided by the British Educational Research Association (2011). These principles were communicated to all project participants and translated into practices to protect individual anonymity and ensure confidentiality. This was particularly important as TERN was a small-scale and very public project in which individual participants might well be identifiable without these measures. Presentation of these data is guided by the same ethical principles in order to preserve anonymity. Thus, in the discussion below, research groups are assigned a colour name; there is no reference to the names for each research group used in the project.

A socio-cultural framing of online communication and collaboration

The TERN project was informed by a socio-cultural approach to professional learning (see, for example, Eraut 2000, Evans *et al.* 2006). These approaches build upon the foundations of communities of practice literature (Lave and Wenger 1991, Wenger 1998), thereby situating professional learning within the context of the workplace: newcomers learn and gain competence through interactions with more experienced colleagues within that workplace. The individual learns through engaging in and contributing to the practices of their workplace communities, and the communities' practices are refined and developed through the participation of the individuals within them (Wenger 1998, p. 7). The research fellows' learning was situated within their participation in their research group and, as with Lave and

Wenger's model of a community of practice, the research mentor initially occupied the role of the expert in relation to the group's communal purpose, which was to develop a research bid. For Wenger, such communities are characterised by three aspects: mutual engagement, a joint enterprise or shared purpose, and a shared repertoire of resources. Members of a community are seen to progress from legitimate peripheral participation, where their participation is limited and prescribed by the group's habitual ways of working, to fuller participation, as they gain competence 'along the lines of technical knowledge and linguistic and cultural knowledges' (Martin 2005, p. 153). In their exit questionnaires, a large number of participants used language in a similar vein to that of the communities of practice literature to describe their learning within the research groups. They reported on their progression from 'peripheral' to 'increased' participation within the research group as their knowledge and confidence of the research area increased, and they related this to their developing identities as researchers.

Embedded within a socio-cultural approach to learning and professional development is a socio-cultural approach to literacy (see, for example, Gee 1996, Cope and Kalantzis 2000). Written language is a key constituent of most learning and, where learning is primarily facilitated through a textually mediated VRE, attention to the use of written language is a vital part of understanding the learning process. Although virtual technologies provide a plethora of affordances to develop multimodal texts (Kress 2003), the TERN research groups' participations within the VRE were overwhelmingly through the written word. Rather than assuming that reading and writing are a discrete set of skills that exist in isolation to any one text, we view literacy in terms of the social practices of participants who are shaped by their social, institutional and cultural contexts: 'literacies identify communities. They entail cultural actors – the writing *for* them and the reading *by* them' (Crook 2005, p. 510) and the researcher needs to focus on 'what is read and what is written, where, how, by whom, why and under what conditions' (Ivanic *et al.* 2009, p. 20). A wide range of personal factors therefore influence the individual's participation with text, including their motivations, values and social relations (Barton and Hamilton 1998). The individual develops habitual ways of using text (literacy practices) that inform/influence/enable their instantiated engagement with a particular text at a particular time, a moment of textual engagement that has been described as a 'literacy event' (Heath 1982). This relationship between literacy practices and literacy events is two-directional: while literacy practices are instantiated in the literacy event, so do literacy events become constituents of the evolving literacy practice (Hamilton 2000).

In relation to the VRE, then, any understanding of how individuals engage with the technology needs to be understood in relation to their previous literacy practices; their broader socio-cultural contexts; the literacy practices (values, attitudes, dispositions, etc.) brought by other members of the group towards this new technology, its tools and the emerging texts; and the context of their TERN research group. This context is shaped by the written content that other group members have contributed. In turn, the possibilities of reading and writing are structured and shaped by the affordances of the VRE. The self-report survey data and interview transcripts provided us with a degree of insight into the literacy practices that research fellows brought with them to the project, and the archive of VRE communications provided evidence of texts mediated by this technology. Together these offered some understanding of participants' use and valuing of the VRE.

The TERN research groups were distinctive entities, carefully constructed for the purposes of the project (for details, see Murray *et al.* 2011), and as such can be seen as artificial constructs. This had repercussions for how participants engaged with and learnt from these communities. There was a schism between two distinct types of learning within the group. On the one hand, research fellows were ostensibly involved with the research groups to learn how to 'become' researchers through purposeful, collaborative engagement towards the development of a research bid, with a more experienced colleague providing mentoring and guidance. There were also indications that research fellows followed a trajectory towards greater involvement within the group as they gained confidence in their 'researcher identities'. This aspect of learning aligned well with the expectations of professional learning detailed above and anticipated through our 'embedded social practices' approach to research capacity-building (Baron 2005). On the other hand, at the point of group creation, there was no shared and habitual repertoire of communication and collaboration practices through which newcomers could learn to participate within the group: all members of the group were, in effect, 'newcomers'. All participants were also positioned as learners in relation to the VRE tools, which were intended to mediate the practices through which participants were learning how to become researchers. This leads into the next area of discussion for this paper: given that all participants were newcomers to the VRE, what factors affected their engagement with this new technology?

Factors influencing individuals' learning to use the TERN VRE

Individuals' existing practices and expertise

Although taking a socio-cultural approach to learning, we also recognise the centrality of the individual's disposition to learning as a key factor in their professional development. Usefully for our argument here, Hodkinson and Hodkinson's (2004) case study of two teachers highlights that even when many aspects of the activity system are the same – for example, the rules of the workplace and the object of learning – individuals' approaches to learning can be significantly different. The importance of the individual's disposition to learning in relation to situated approaches to professional learning is further theorised by Evans *et al.* (2006) and Fuller and Unwin (2004): they develop the concept of the individual's 'learning territory', a concept that takes account of the personal backgrounds, prior education and professional experiences, and aspirations of the individual: 'every individual has, and has had, access to a (unique) range of learning opportunities which make up their learning territory' (Fuller and Unwin 2004, p. 133). This appreciation of the unique backgrounds, values and motivations of the individual is important to how we make sense of the ways in which the TERN research fellows engaged with and positioned themselves in relation to learning how to use the VRE.

An individual's existing level of familiarity and competence with technology and online environments was not the overriding factor determining their engagement with the VRE. In fact, the TERN research fellows and mentors brought a broad range of technological expertise to the project. Technology is a dominant part of many academics' lives, and self-report data completed by participants for the mapping exercise at the start of the project suggested that participants had relatively high levels of technical expertise: for example, 78% of participants (29/37) used online discussion fora frequently or occasionally, and 78% had previously used virtual learning environments (31/40). In his external evaluation of the pilot project, Gardner (2009) suggested that this existing expertise 'scotch[ed]' the possible explanation that problems with the technology may have arisen from research fellows' unfamiliarity with online environments. The appearance and the design structure of the VRE were new to all participants, but the kinds of tools it contained were familiar to most. The challenge here is therefore: to explore the ways in which individuals' literacy practices, the habitual ways they had developed to engage with similar kinds of texts, benefitted or hindered their engagement with the VRE; and to understand why their pre-existing expertise with similar technologies did not transfer unproblematically to effective, ongoing engagement with the VRE.

Laterza *et al.* postulated that:

> any attempt to explain a particular pattern of VRE use as the 'result' of other human variables is bound to fail, as the set of tools and functions (and their real and perceived deficiencies) shapes practices as much as it is shaped by them. (2007, p. 262)

Within our dataset there were counter-intuitive examples where participants who were 'new' to the virtual tools engaged more proactively and positively in learning new practices than those who brought established ways of using this type of virtual tool. But at the start of the project we had assumed that pre-existing expertise with similar technologies would provide a valuable resource for research fellows in gaining competence with the VRE. This was the case for some participants who navigated and utilised the new VRE with ease and for some who successfully mobilised knowledge from other virtual learning environments or computer applications. For example, the research mentor of the turquoise group brought extensive technical expertise to the project and, early within her group's VRE-mediated collaboration, inserted hyperlinked text into a newly formed wiki, while a research fellow in this group set out ideas for an initial research proposal on the wiki, creating a folder and uploading a relevant document to the resources area and posting an announcement explaining what she/he had done. These actions suggest that these individuals were able to transfer their practices from other contexts to the new VRE.

However, existing expertise appeared at times also to be a hindrance to learning new literacy practices, rather than being of benefit through supporting the transfer of skills from one literacy event to another. Our literacy practices are, in part, shaped by our earlier interactions with text (Gee 1996, Barton and Hamilton 1998), and therefore one's engagement with any new technology will be influenced or informed, in part, by the design and affordances of previous technologies that one has used. The literacy practices that a participant might bring to a textually mediated new technology can clash against the literacy demands of that new technology. Some TERN participants were familiar with more advanced technologies, or technologies that they considered to be superior to the TERN VRE, and this limited their motivation to engage with this technology. For instance, one research mentor was critical of the design of the wiki page because the 'save' button was located at the bottom of the textbox rather than at the top of the page. She considered this to be inferior to the design of the wiki that she habitually used, and therefore rejected this wiki as poorly designed and of limited use.

Training on how to use the VRE tools

All participants were invited to attend three training sessions focused on using the new VRE. Some research fellows were critical of the need for this kind of provision; one participant commented in his/her exit questionnaire: 'I was quite au fait with all of those systems and I could use them quite easily: there were some days when I was in workshops thinking, why, you know, when I'm tired and hungry, why am I here'. For some other research fellows, the workshops were invaluable in providing the opportunity to experiment with new technologies and to receive guidance from a tutor: the workshops provided a context within which they could build their confidence with and trust in the technology (Szecsy *et al.* 2005).

Powell and Orme (2011) highlight the stress caused by the academic imperative to do research. TERN research fellows were subjected to similar imperatives to develop their research activities and, simultaneously, to develop a new set of technology skills through which their professional learning would be mediated. For some participants, therefore, the introduction of the VRE stimulated an emotional response that had a negative impact upon their learning, particularly as some participants felt overwhelmed by the challenges of learning a new technology. For example, in the first training session one research fellow dramatically leapt from his/her chair within a few minutes of logging on and announced that she/he had broken the entire VRE. For these individuals, engaging with the technology was stressful, and any setback probably had significant consequences upon their future engagement. One research fellow reflected in his/her exit questionnaire, that she/he 'lost her nerve' following the temporary loss of some of her files. An additional factor emerging from exit interviews related to the visibility of participants' learning to other members of their research group. This was because the learning was situated in an online environment where live tools allowed participants to see mistakes which their colleagues made. While this was not problematic for all, some participants felt exposed. Some participants felt discouraged from identifying themselves as novices in relation to the various worksite tools: for example, on the exit questionnaire one research fellow reflected that 'I believe the people in our group didn't know each other well enough, socially, to openly and freely post things on the VRE', whilst another similarly reflected 'the VLE [*sic*] did not really work for us, since we were all rather new to the area of research and posting on the VLE seemed to put people off'.

Furthermore, there appeared to be issues around negotiating identity. Within the research groups, individuals were negotiating their identity in relation to their useful expertise and knowledge for the content of the research proposal being developed, and in relation to the technical tools designed to mediate the collaboration of this bid. Being a novice in relation to the technical tools, which would be very visible to other group members through the VRE, risked marginalising the expertise that one brought to the group in relation to content knowledge.

Relevance of VRE to the project

Socio-cultural approaches to literacy tend to stress the importance of developing competences with the literacy demands of the workplace through learning contextualised by the real purposes and contexts of the workplace (Ivanic *et al.* 2009), but these data suggest that there may be value in providing decontextualised opportunities for participants to experiment with the tools that mediate the workplace literacy demands. There was a tension in the TERN project between the principles of 'situated learning', which informed the design of the pilot, and the need to gain proficiency with the tools needed to mediate this situated learning. It may have been beneficial to some participants to have set up 'dummy' worksites within which participants could experiment with the tools: a pedagogic approach that moves away from the principle of developing expertise through situated purposeful activities. Any dummy activities would also have required an additional time commitment from participants. To gain proficiency in a new technology requires some investment of time, whether one is an experienced user of technology or a relative novice (Wilson *et al.* 2007). Furthermore, this investment of time is likely to be ongoing as one develops familiarity with the available tools – as one participant commented in her exit questionnaire: 'I found most [VRE tools] valuable, but had to remind myself how to use them all!'

The 'fitness for purpose' of the VRE was critiqued by a considerable number of research fellows and their mentors in exit interviews and on the exit questionnaire. The reliability of the VRE was compromised by ongoing problems with logging into the system: the technology had not yet reached a point in its development where it could easily cope with high numbers of users (a factor that was not anticipated by the TERN management group). Initial logging-on problems caused some participants to lose trust in the VRE's effectiveness in mediating communicative and collaborative working practices and reduced the perceived credibility of the technology. The green group's confidence with the technology was destroyed by another technical problem. The research mentor initiated a wiki to serve the purpose of providing a 'first stab at our research proposal', but this work was then lost. One research fellow pragmatically reflected on the exit questionnaire that: 'The wiki – we started with enthusiasm but somehow everything got erased (not sure how this happened) so we need to start again and discuss between us how to make sure we don't press the wrong buttons'. However, other group members were driven by this experience to take a decisive move away from the VRE to alternative technologies.

Attention has been given to the effects of the 'information explosion' (see, for example, Feather 2008), but for many there has been a corresponding 'technology explosion'. As one research fellow explained in the exit questionnaire, there was no point in trying to understand even more software: 'I don't think I can add another substantial layer of communication to my life. I'm just too full!' From this perspective, the VRE represents just another form of technology, and new technologies emerge in the shadow of older technologies. Many of the individuals involved with TERN had previously invested considerable time learning to navigate technologies that were now defunct or that had proved unfit for purpose. It is therefore not surprising if they approached (another) new technology with scepticism and reluctance. That no research groups established ongoing practices mediated by the VRE can be seen to demonstrate the limited value that this technology was seen to offer their group. All groups evolved communicative and collaborative practices mediated by more familiar kinds of technology rather than utilising the affordances offered by the VRE.

Earlier in this paper, we argued that individuals' engagement with the VRE was contextualised by their TERN research group. This took place in relation both to the evolving utilisation of the technology and to the textual content of the site. The usefulness of the VRE to research groups was also dependent, therefore, upon the content which group members contributed to the site. At the start of the project,

TERN provided each research group with a set of tools within the VRE worksites, but these were unpopulated with content. The turquoise group very quickly began to post content onto their site, as discussed above, but some groups failed to develop content within the VRE, thereby rendering the technology purposeless. It is possible that the worksites may have become much richer learning environments if they had been populated with relevant content; for example, useful resources and recent group discussions. This content would have encouraged group members to participate and, therefore, learn through engaging with the technology: without content, participants were unlikely to engage; without engagement, the sites were unlikely to become populated with useful content.

The challenges of developing shared practices within a newly formed community

Individuals from the turquoise group rapidly established repertoires of practices mediated by the VRE tools, but these did not become established across the group. The turquoise group's use of the VRE had ceased within two months of the first research group meeting, and they reverted to the use of more familiar technologies: namely, email and Microsoft *Word* documents with tracked changes. Without a whole group commitment, the VRE could not effectively support communication and collaboration.

As Wenger (1998, p. 100) explains, participation should provide access 'to mutual engagement with other members, to their actions and their negotiation of the enterprise, and the repertoire in use'. Individual behaviours with the technology cannot lead to 'mutual engagement' if other participants are not reading and/or responding to an individual's writings so that the individual can develop a repertoire of practices mediated by the VRE. For example, writing using the wiki or making announcements with the announcements tool cannot become useful to the group as a whole unless they are accessed and utilised by more members.

Jarman (2005, p. 337) refers to the need for a 'critical mass' – 'the use of the technology to a level where it is a natural part of the processes of the team' – and argues that:

> collaborative technologies require a very high proportion of users to use the technology for it to be effective. Failure to achieve critical mass will mean the particular technology has not been adopted and continued use of the technology will hinder the team. (Jarman 2005, p. 337)

Individuals' learning territories are highly relevant to understanding their initial approach to the new technology, but the longer-term effectiveness of technology in supporting communication and collaboration is increasingly dependent upon the behaviours of the research group as a whole.

As we have explored earlier in this paper, in relation to their developing a research bid, the research groups seemed to conform to Wenger's (1998) conceptual architecture of a learning community: research fellows moved progressively from peripheral to legitimate participation through their interactions with the community (in physical and virtual spaces) and, through participation, developed the knowledge and confidence necessary to grow their research identities. The role of the research mentor was designed to provide initial expertise and guidance to the group but then to allow the community of practice to evolve over time, rather than seeking to control this process.

In relation to the group's 'learning' around the technical tools of the VRE, a very different architecture emerged. Within these constructed-for-purpose research groups, there was no existing expertise and there were no established working practices. Whereas the TLRP research project teams had worked together prior to establishing their use of the VRE (Laterza *et al.* 2007), because of the time-frame within which the ESRC asked for the TERN project to be conducted its research groups began to work collaboratively within the VRE at the same time as their initial formation as a community. This 'newness' of the community emerged as an important dynamic when exploring individuals' engagement with the technology. As we discussed above, group members had different notions of how the different tools might be used and which purposes they might serve. Research mentors were not expected to provide leadership in the uses of the new technology, and besides, in all but one research group, the research mentor did not feel that they were a technology 'expert' within the group. The two examples below illustrate some of the tensions that emerged within the groups: both these groups allowed individuals to develop their own repertoire of VRE use rather than requiring that all individuals conform to an agreed group-wide repertoire.

As with all the research groups, the blue group met for the first time at Workshop One and attended an initial coaching session on the VRE. Immediately following this event a flurry of activity took place within their VRE worksite. Initial activity focused primarily on building upon the face-to-face discussions that had taken place at the first workshop. For example, one research fellow uploaded a document through the resources tool and then posted an announcement which informed other group members that she/he had uploaded 'a summary of the key emerging questions [as identified at Workshop 1]' through which she/he hoped to summarise 'what you all perceived to be the key areas of discussion!' Following the second workshop, another research fellow used the discussion forum as a tool to record conceptual issues arising at this workshop and she/he, again, used the announcements tool to inform other group members of the discussions' location. A third research fellow extensively used the wiki tool with the intention of further stimulating discussion and bringing together the group's ideas. Both the research mentor and the research fellow who used the resources and announcements tools following the first workshop posted comments to this wiki text, but other members did not visibly collaborate in this activity. This example suggests that individuals were developing their own working practices rather than group-wide working practices being negotiated. The announcements tool was used to direct participants to recent activity on the worksite, but neither the wiki nor the discussion forum referenced each other or referred to the initial document stored in the resources area, although the purposes of these three texts were broadly similar. It appears that activities were not effectively shared across the group because there were no agreed practices through which these kinds of activities took place.

The green group, in contrast, regularly used only one tool within the VRE: the chat tool. The chat tool is a real-time communication tool, similar to other online chat tools such as instant messaging. The text develops in a linear form, with the text chronologically sequenced on the screen with more recently inputted text visible at the top of the screen. The standard setting for the chat tool in this VRE is to display messages inputted over the past three days, unless this has been manually changed by the registered user, which means that the reader is not automatically aware of messages that have been posted more than three days ago. The green group used the chat tool for different purposes, including the discussion of both practical and conceptual content and for social and team-building purposes. The tool has no means of arranging these discussions thematically. Therefore, although the chat tool is the most user-friendly for the 'writer' in relation to the posting of text into the worksite, it is the least accessible for the 'reader' who needs to work through all the postings to find what is relevant to him/her. As one group member reflected on the exit questionnaire: 'material was often difficult to find and we abandoned its use'. The navigation problems experienced by the green group were exacerbated by individuals using the same tool for very different purposes. Additionally, the green group mentor preferred to distribute resources via email rather than uploading these to the VRE. Although this content was cross-referenced within the VRE, it required participants to use email, rather than the VRE, to access relevant resources, thereby further reducing the use-value of the VRE.

Rather than these groups developing a shared repertoire of practices to mediate collaboration and communication, evidence from both groups suggests that individuals pursued their own preferred individual practices and that this generated challenges for the potential of the VRE to support collaboration and communication. It is therefore not surprising that other tools might have been seen as being more effective ways of supporting collaboration, although this may relate as much to the group's behaviours as to the actual affordances of the available tools. Carmichael and Burchmore (2010) suggest that this kind of 'piecemeal' adoption of technology across the higher education sector is caused by the imbalance between 'enablers' (i.e. in relation to this paper, the affordances of available technologies) and 'drivers' (i.e. the needs and purposes of groups and individuals). Within the TERN project, there were, for most participants, no clear relationships between the drivers of developing a collaborative research bid and the value of the VRE as an 'enabler'. For Wenger (1998, p. 82), elements of the available repertoire (and we include within this, the possible affordances of the VRE) 'gain their coherence not in and of themselves ..., but from the fact that they belong to the practice of a community pursuing an enterprise'. In relation to the newly formed nature of the TERN research groups, this raises questions of how practices within a group become habitualised. How is, or should, a balance be generated between the individuals' preferred practices and the development of an agreed set of practices across the group? For Wenger (1998, p. 87), 'practices evolve as shared histories of learning', a 'combination of participation and reification intertwined over time'; but, in relation to TERN, there was no shared history, only a gathering together of individuals into a newly formed community whose members, even though they shared a communal purpose, had unique learning territories.

Reflecting back on their participation in the project, some participants recognised that their group became more effective at collaborating over time – comments from exit interviews included: 'in some sense, it feels like a genuine collaboration which has emerged because the interests and expertise fit. But it's taken some time to get to that point!' and 'it took us a while to establish a more democratic approach, but we did eventually'. The dynamics of the groups changed over time with, in most cases, the research mentor moving from a central position within the group to a more peripheral participation as other group members gained confidence and began to lead the work. The emerging leadership by some individuals links to the establishment of group working practices, which was not always led by research mentors. As noted, while coaching and ongoing technical support on the VRE were provided to all research groups, it was anticipated that the group's working practices within the VRE would evolve democratically. The research mentors of different groups adopted different roles in relation to their group's use of the VRE. For example, the blue group's research mentor, whilst identifying himself/herself as a novice in relation to the technology, provided expert input in relation to the content of the discussions and in the provision of regular positive feedback, and mirrored in a supportive manner the practices and tools that the particular individuals in the group chose to use. This proved to be a complex role, straddling the identities of a technical novice and a research expert. For example, one response of a research mentor in a Chat Room was prefaced by: 'I'm trying to get a hang of this new technology'. The majority of this mentor's written contributions began by reference to the medium used but rapidly moved towards the substantive focus of the group.

No groups appointed a technological 'expert' or 'leader'. It would be interesting in future projects to explore whether strong leadership is more effective than the distributed democratic approach adopted by TERN at establishing a shared repertoire of practices. Groups might have benefitted from leadership in relation to such group protocols.

For example, in face-to-face discussions with group members, concerns were raised about ownership and copyright in relation to collaboration and the sharing of ideas. Carmichael and Youdell (2007) explore the ethical issues related to the moral rights of contributors and the ownership of online content and recommend that research groups establish and publicise explicit protocols. The absence of these kinds of protocol within the research groups could have discouraged some participants from engaging with the online tools for fear that their 'ideas' might be 'stolen'.

Strategic leadership was also needed in coordinating some activities that required real-time communication. The online chat tool only worked effectively if participants were available at the same time, and few groups managed to coordinate the time for this kind of collaboration. For example, two research fellows made the following observations in their exit questionnaires:

> Chatroom was valuable at first, but frustrating as no one else from the group was chatting!

> A couple of conversations we had were positively glacial in their speed, since person A would not know that person B had read their message and would then go off to do something else, and by the time person A went back to check, 15 minutes had elapsed since person B's response ... and so on.

In relation to the need for effective coordination of group participation in online environments, Shapiro and Hughes (2010, p. 62) observe that, 'the posting of one message that is not responded to can lead to the individual posting it feeling totally unrecognised or ostracised'. The lack of coordination in the use of research tools can have negative social effects upon the developing social relationships between group members. The experiences of learning with the group become part of the individual's learning territory and influence their future literacy practices.

In established communities of practice, leadership and authority may have been provided by 'old timers' who had a history of participation within the community

(Wenger 1998). While this was possible within the TERN groups in relation to the focus upon the research bid because research mentors with significant expertise and experience had been allocated to each group, this did not occur in relation to a technology to which all participants were 'newcomers'.

The importance of facilitation from within and/or outside the community

The TERN research groups were not self-contained, but existed across the business of day-to-day teacher education and were impacted upon not only by the micro-politics of the Schools of Education within each university but also by the larger political climate of educational research, an issue explored in more depth by Murray *et al.* (2012). Wenger (1998, p. 78) calls attention to how the day-to-day reality of participants' engagement with the community of practice is constrained by their position within a broader system and the pervasive influence of the institution that employs them. Certainly these pressures were acute for many participants who engaged with TERN. For example, many participants recognised that they needed to invest time in 'getting to grips' with the VRE; that is, they needed time to be learners within the new technology before they could become proficient users. However, this time was rarely available and, in their exit questionnaires, many participants expressed regrets that they had not had more time to devote to TERN in general. This finding is not unique to the experience of TERN: in their evaluation of AERS in Scotland, Wilson *et al.* (2007, p. 296) found that participants employed in the higher education sector were initially 'slow to devote time to engaging with the virtual space', in part because this kind of investment of time was not valued by their institution. Carmichael (2009, p. 21) recommends that the provision of time to develop technological abilities should be supported by peers, supervisors and superiors: 'This allows individuals to devote time to networking activities on a regular basis rather than intermittently'. Where inadequate time is available to gain proficiency in new technical tools, it is unsurprising that users default to those tools with which they are already familiar; without adequate time, the value and usefulness of the VRE are unable to emerge (Laterza *et al.* 2007).

The problem of insufficient time can be seen to extend more generally to participants' opportunities for professional development. This is a serious issue within teacher education (Sikes 2006, Murray 2008), where the work of many teacher educators is dominated by teaching, management and partnership work, and is also a relevant issue for other practice-based academic disciplines. For example, Boyd and Lawley identify similar challenges within nurse education and recommend that:

> higher education institutions need to back up the rhetoric of support and development with staffing resources that enable some protected time for new lecturers so that they are able to focus more systematically on their professional development including scholarship and research activity. (2009, p. 299)

Within social work, Orme and Powell (2008, p. 998) advise that, 'social work academics should ensure that written into their personal development plans are training opportunities in specific research methods, research supervision and membership of doctoral research supervision teams'. We would argue that central to any allocation of 'resource' is a facilitator or mentor, an 'old-timer' (to borrow the language of communities of practice) who is able to guide the newcomer. While the practices of professional development within TERN were primarily occurring within the research groups, a champion from outside these communities may have been able to 'catalyse' this process; that is, increase the value that an individual gained from available capacity-building structures and professional development practices (Fowler and Procter 2008). What was needed was the provision of good role-models, who inspired a sense of purpose, provided clear direction and injected others with enthusiasm (Holligan et al. 2011, p. 713).

In relation to the TLRP research groups, Laterza et al. (2007, pp. 264–265) identified the 'need for effective and continued management and for continuing induction of new users into the online environment'. In AERS, each of the projects was led by a key person who acted as a facilitator (Wilson et al. 2007) or what Laterza et al. (2007) would describe as a 'VRE champion'. This key person provided expertise, motivation and brokerage to support the research group's engagement with the new technology. In relation to online professional development in Australia, Henderson (2007, p. 171) stresses the importance of 'community brokers' to facilitate individuals' learning and to engage with other members in mutual, accountable and negotiable ways. This brokerage is often short term but it is vital at the start of the group's engagement with the technology: 'in order to achieve [a] supportive culture … [as] participants need to feel that their participation is important' (Henderson 2007, p. 171).

Conclusions

In this paper we have adopted a socio-cultural approach to professional learning, therefore recognising that individuals' behaviours and emerging practices need to be understood in relation to learning motivation, group dynamics and institutional climate. The TERN research groups can be understood as communities of practice in that they represented mutual engagement towards a joint enterprise facilitated by a shared repertoire of resources (Wenger 1998). These communities of practice did not exist in isolation, but were also influenced and shaped by the wider contexts of participants' departments, institutions, professional responsibilities and broader lives.

The TERN research groups were constructed for purpose within this necessarily fast-paced pilot project, and this created particular challenges related to learning within newly formed communities of practice lacking both shared histories of meaning and habitualised ways of working. While the TERN pilot project successfully achieved its overall aims, remedial action was considered necessary to upskill TERN participants in use of the VRE tools. This reduced the time available for individual, face-to-face interaction in the research groups, which had been identified by participants as particularly valuable spaces for cross-institutional communication and collaboration. Also individual and group dissatisfaction and/or frustration with the VRE may have impacted on some groups' learning and progress more than others, accounting for some of the differentiated outcomes of the project. A major challenge facing the introduction of a new technology is how to balance the purposes of the immediate activity with the need to gain proficiency with the technological tools employed to mediate this work.

Patterns of use within the VRE demonstrated some improvisation and innovation, but there was a lack of persistence across all groups. Resistance to learning how to use the VRE was influenced by participants' learning 'territories' and previous literacy practices: some participants were sceptical about the affordances of the VRE because they tended to use technologies that they considered to be superior; some participants lacked confidence in their abilities to use this new technology; and some participants were concerned about the visibility of their learning to other group members. Importantly, the VRE was unable to gain credibility and purpose if research groups did not generate shared practices and populate the worksite with relevant content that would have provided the purpose for its use. Overall, as with the AERS project in Scotland, conclusions from the first year of TERN suggest that, 'establishing the virtual space as a "normal" means of communication, of learning, and of collaborative working remains very much an aspiration' (Wilson *et al.* 2007, p. 296).

Despite the limitations of the research presented here, we believe that our findings raise valuable and more general issues for the future design and deployment of new technologies in academic learning. With the benefits of hindsight, this pilot project would have benefitted from more time, in relation to both individual learning and the evolution of group-wide repertoires of shared practices. A more effective balance might also have been struck between the VRE as an 'enabler' (Carmichael and Burchmore 2010) and the groups' emerging practices as a 'driver'. The VRE was introduced as part of the design of the project rather than emerging as a response to the groups' ways of collaborating and communicating, which created an artificiality to the technology and meant that it was never fully integrated into any of the groups' working practices. Based on our experience in the TERN project, we would also suggest that successful engagement with new technologies in future academic communities of practice might well benefit from a communal purpose for and shared commitment to adopting the technology, agreed group protocols about its use and the deployment of 'champions' to inspire, motivate and support users.

Acknowledgements

The research was funded by the ESRC under research grant RES-069-25-0008.

Note

1. We should mention that an additional and far more successful worksite was also set up for all TERN participants at the start of the project, administered and managed by one member of the network who has established clear protocols for the use of different tools. It contains regularly updated announcements, news items and access to relevant resources. With the TERN project now in its fourth year of existence, this worksite remains available to and is used heavily by project participants. The value of the content and its clear location as a set of texts posted within this VRE has attracted far more engagement from TERN participants than the examples reflected upon above in relation to engagement with research group worksites.

References

Baron, S., 2005. TLRP's phase 2 research capacities building strategy. *Research intelligence*, 93, 14–17.

Barton, D. and Hamilton, M., 1998. *Local literacies: a study of reading and writing in one community*. London: Routledge.

Boyd, P. and Lawley, L., 2009. Becoming a lecturer in nurse education: the workplace learning of clinical experts as newcomers. *Learning in health and social care*, 8 (4), 292–300.

British Educational Research Association, 2011. *Ethical guidelines for educational research 2011* [online]. London: British Educational Research Association. Available from: http://www.bera.ac.uk/guidelines [Accessed 28 June 2012].

Carmichael, P., 2009. *A social and professional network for early career researchers in education: ESRC end of award report.* Swindon: ESRC.

Carmichael, P. and Burchmore, H., 2010. Social software and academic practice: post-graduate students as co-designers of Web 2.0 tools. *Internet and higher education*, 13 (4), 233–241.

Carmichael, P. and Youdell, D., 2007. Using virtual collaboration environments for education research: some ethical considerations. *Research intelligence*, 100, 26–29.

Carmichael, P., *et al.*, 2006. Sakai: a virtual research environment for education research. *Research intelligence*, 96, 18.

Conole, G. and Alevizou, P., 2010. *A literature review of the use of Web 2.0 tools in higher education: a report commissioned by the Higher Education Academy.* Milton Keynes: The Open University.

Cope, B. and Kalantzis, M., eds., 2000. *Multiliteracies: literacy learning and the design of social futures.* London: Routledge.

Crook, C., 2005. Addressing research at the intersection of academic literacies and new technology. *International journal of educational research*, 43 (7–8), 509–518.

Eraut, M., 2000. Non-formal learning and tacit knowledge in professional working. *British journal of educational psychology*, 70 (1), 113–136.

Evans, L., *et al.*, 2006. *Improving workplace learning.* London: Routledge.

Feather, J., 2008. *The information society: a study of continuity and change.* London: Facet.

Fowler, Z. and Procter, R., 2008. *'Mapping the Ripples': a taster.* London: TLRP.

Fuller, A. and Unwin, L., 2004. Expansive learning environments: integrating organisational and personal development. *In*: H. Rainbird, A. Fuller, and A. Munro, eds. *Workplace learning in context.* London: Routledge, 126–144.

Gardner, J., 2009. *Evaluation of the Teacher Education Research Network (TERN) 2008–09: Economic and Social Research Council (ESRC) external examiner's report.* Swindon: ESRC.

Gee, J.P., 1996. *Social linguistics and literacies: ideology in discourses.* New York: Falmer.

Goodfellow, R. and Lea, M., 2007. *Challenging e-learning in the university: a literacies perspective.* Maidenhead: Open University Press.

Hamilton, M., 2000. Expanding the New Literacy studies: using photographs to explore literacy as social practice. *In*: D. Barton, M. Hamilton, and R. Ivanic, eds. *Situated literacies: reading and writing in context.* London: Routledge, 16–34.

Heath, S.B., 1982. Protean shapes in literacy events: ever-shifting oral and literate traditions. *In*: D. Tannen, ed. *Spoken and written language: exploring orality and literacy.* Norwood, NJ: Ablex, 91–117.

Henderson, M., 2007. Sustaining online teacher professional development through community design. *Campus-wide information systems*, 24 (3), 162–173.

Hodkinson, P. and Hodkinson, H., 2004. The significance of individuals' dispositions in workplace learning: a case study of two teachers. *Journal of work and education*, 17 (2), 167–182.

Holligan, C., Wilson, M., and Humes, W., 2011. Research cultures in English and Scottish university education departments: an exploratory study of academic staff perceptions. *British educational research journal*, 37 (4), 713–734.

Ivanic, R., *et al.*, 2009. *Improving learning in college.* London: Routledge.

Jarman, R., 2005. When success isn't everything – case studies of two virtual teams. *Group decision and negotiation*, 14 (4), 333–354.

Kress, G., 2003. *Literacy in the new media age.* London: Routledge.

Laterza, V., Carmichael, P., and Procter, R., 2007. The doubtful guest?: a virtual research environment for education. *Technology, pedagogy and education*, 16 (3), 249–267.

Lave, J. and Wenger, E., 1991. *Situated learning: legitimate peripheral participation.* Cambridge, UK: Cambridge University Press.

Lea, M.R., 2004. Academic literacies: a pedagogy for course design. *Studies in higher education*, 29 (6), 739–756.

Martin, D., 2005. Communities of practice and learning communities: do bilingual co-workers learn in community? In: D. Barton and K. Tusting, eds. *Beyond communities of practice: language, power and social context.* New York: Cambridge University Press, 139–157.

Murray, J., 2008. Teacher educators' induction into higher education: work-based learning in the micro communities of teacher education. *European journal of teacher education,* 31 (2), 117–133.

Murray, J., *et al.*, 2011. *The Teacher Education Research Network (TERN): building research capacity in the North West region of England: ESRC project final report – RES-069-25-0008* [online]. Swindon: ESRC. Available from: http://www.esrc.ac.uk/my-esrc/grants/RES-069-25-0008/outputs/Read/a6c2141a-d175-4d33-9bdd-ea2b8311078e [Accessed 28 June 2012].

Murray, J., *et al.*, 2012. Reorientation and teacher education in England. *In*: R. Adamson, J. Nixon, and F. Su, eds. *The reorientation of higher education: challenging the east–west dichotomy.* New York: Springer, 184–206.

Orme, J. and Powell, J., 2008. Building research capacity in social work: process and issues. *The British journal of social work,* 38 (5), 988–1008.

Powell, J. and Orme, J., 2011. Increasing the confidence and competence of social work researchers: what works? *The British journal of social work,* 41 (8), 1566–1585.

Rees, G., *et al.*, 2007. Research-capacity building, professional learning and the social practices of educational research. *British educational research journal,* 33 (5), 761–781.

Ross, J., 2011. Traces of self: online reflective practices and performances in higher education. *Teaching in higher education,* 16 (1), 113–126.

Shapiro, J.J. and Hughes, S.K., 2010. The challenges of culture and community in online academic environments. *In*: K.E. Rudestam and J. Schoenholtz-Read, eds. *Handbook of online learning.* 2nd ed. Thousand Oaks, CA: Sage, 57–90.

Sikes, P., 2006. Working in a 'new' university: in the shadow of the Research Assessment Exercise. *Studies in higher education,* 31 (5), 234–252.

Street, B.V., ed., 2005. *Literacies across educational contexts: mediating learning and teaching.* Philadelphia, PA: Caslon Publishing.

Szecsy, E.M., Danzig, A.B., and Gonzalez, J.M., 2005. The use of information and communication technology (ICT) to encourage reflection, interaction and collaboration for innovation and professional growth in higher and adult education. *Paper presented at the annual conference of the Northeastern Educational Research Association,* 19–21 October, Kerhonkson, NY.

Wenger, E., 1998. *Communities of practice: learning, meaning and identity.* Cambridge, UK: Cambridge University Press.

Wilson, A., *et al.*, 2007. Using a virtual research environment to support new models of collaborative and participative research in Scottish education. *Technology, pedagogy and education,* 16 (3), 289–304.

Pushing the envelope on what is known about professional development: the virtual school experience

Nancy Fichtman Dana, Kara Dawson, Rachel Wolkenhauer and Desi Krell

School of Teaching and Learning, University of Florida, USA

The purpose of this study was to understand the ways virtual school teachers experienced professional development framed as a year-long collaborative action research endeavour. These virtual school teachers taught completely online courses for a large virtual school and did not reside within the same geographical location. Thus, the professional development was supported by the use of various synchronous and asynchronous technology tools. This study provides insights into what constitutes powerful online professional learning opportunities not only for virtual school teachers, but for their traditional face-to-face school counterparts, as well as the ways synchronous and asynchronous technology tools can be utilized to scaffold professional learning.

Introduction

Enrolments in virtual schools, defined as organizations that deliver education entirely or partially via online methods, are on the rise (Ferdig *et al.* 2009). As of 2012, over 1.8 million students in the United States enrolled in at least one online course and 250,000 students enrolled full-time in virtual schools (International Association for K–12 Online Learning 2012). While full-time virtual schooling is currently most prevalent in North America (Cavanaugh *et al.* 2009), online learning is growing rapidly in education worldwide (Greenwood *et al.* 2011). Numerous countries – including, but not limited to, Mexico, New Zealand, Australia, China and Singapore – have developed initiatives to increase online learning opportunities (Barbour *et al.* 2011).

As the enterprise of virtual schooling and online learning continues to grow, so does the need to cultivate programmes of professional development for teachers who work in the virtual school context (Rice 2009). While the growth of virtual schools and online learning necessitates that attention be given to the professional development of virtual school teachers, little is known about what constitutes powerful professional learning for this growing group of individuals (Dawley *et al.* 2010) despite growing global interest in preparing educators for virtual teaching (Barbour *et al.* 2011). In addition, common professional development practices in traditional face-to-face school contexts seldom provide a strong model for the ways meaningful professional development might be enacted (Killion and Pinata 2011). Hence, as models of professional development are considered for virtual school teachers and others teaching online, it is critical to understand the pitfalls associated with the ways traditional professional development has been delivered in face-to-face classroom contexts and to cultivate models of professional development that align with strong, research-based models of professional development rather than common but ineffective practices.

One strong, research-based model of professional development that has proved effective is action research. Simply stated, action research (also referred to as practitioner inquiry, teacher inquiry or teacher research) is defined as the systematic, intentional study by educators of their own professional practice (Cochran-Smith and Lytle 1993, 2009). Inquiring professionals seek out change by reflecting on their practice. They do this by engaging in a cyclical process of posing questions, collecting data to gain insights into their questions, analysing the data along with reading relevant literature, taking action to make changes in practice based on new understandings developed during action research and sharing findings with others (Dana and Yendol-Hoppey 2009).

Based on the longevity of the practitioner research movement as well as its strong research base, the systematic study of teachers' own practice is a concept that has gained increasing popularity as a professional development model in traditional face-to-face classroom contexts in nations across the globe (Somekh and Zeichner 2009). For example, López-Pastor *et al.* (2011), in a study of their action research work group in Spain, indicated that educators engaged in action research over the group's 15 years have enhanced practice, increased knowledge, elevated collaboration and cultivated stronger school–university partnerships. Similarly, Toomey *et al.* (2005) discussed how practitioner research has played an important role in improving university–school relations in one Australian context, thus positively impacting both in-service teacher practices and pre-service teacher development. In Sweden, Hardy and Rönnerman (2011) described how a group of teachers engaged in action research through a university initiative overtook the project and expanded collaboration across five schools since 2005; consequently, 'by focusing on the issues ... and critically analysing their work together, all teachers involved better understand their practice' (2011, p. 467). Furthermore, other nations that have been reluctant to adopt practitioner research are now increasing efforts to embrace it as a form of professional development, addressing growing demand for it in Austria (Altrichter and Posch 2010) and integration into teacher education in China (Bai 2009) and Pakistan (Halai 2011).

Also gaining in popularity are online teacher professional development initiatives (Dede 2006). Many of these initiatives tap into benefits of online learning such as opportunities for increased interaction, connection with experts around the world and reflection (Appana 2008). Such online professional development initiatives are occurring at local (Spicer and Dede 2006) and national/international levels with many positive outcomes (Dede *et al.* 2009). Some of these online professional development initiatives are designed to support teachers as they transition to online teaching. For example, the Ministry of Education Virtual Learning Network in New Zealand is investing heavily to bring online learning to rural schools in the country and an associated online professional development course helps prepare teachers to teach online (Dabner *et al.* 2012). Teachers in other countries – including, but not limited to, Canada, Singapore and Australia – also receive online professional development about how to teach online (Barbour *et al.* 2011).

The documented effectiveness of action research as a professional development model for traditional face-to-face classroom teachers as well as initiatives to develop online professional learning opportunities for educators combine to offer a promising professional development model with potential to meet the unique needs of virtual school teachers.

Therefore, the purpose of this study was to understand the ways virtual school teachers describe their experience with professional development when it is framed as a year-long collaborative practitioner research endeavour supported by the use of various synchronous and asynchronous technology tools. Following a brief review of the literature on professional development in general, and action research and virtual teacher professional development in particular, we describe the virtual school action research professional development programme experienced by the participants in this study. Next, we detail the methodology and findings from this study. We end this paper with insights gained from this study about what constitutes powerful professional learning opportunities for not only virtual school teachers, but also their traditional face-to-face school counterparts.

Review of the literature: teacher professional development, action research and virtual school teachers

Historically, the most prominent way that professional learning for teachers who work in a traditional face-to-face school has been actualized in the United States is as an event – a workshop delivered on an in-service day when teachers work but students have a holiday (Lieberman 1995, Sparks and Hirsch 1997, Cochran-Smith and Lytle 1999). In Australia and throughout Europe, professional learning has taken on a similar form as a one-day event (Moss 2008, Lipowski *et al.* 2011, Sugrue 2011), and it can be voluntary, requiring teachers to pay out of their own pockets (Sugrue 2011), or compulsory (Lipowski *et al.* 2011). In these workshops, teachers often learn about new strategies, approaches and pedagogy from an outside expert, and then they are expected to return to their classrooms and independently implement new knowledge.

Experts in the area of teacher professional development recognize the limitations of this traditional model. For example, Borko (2004, p. 4) refers to such events as 'fragmented, intellectually superficial' seminars. Furthermore, Barnett (2002) and Opfer and Pedder (2011) assert that such seminars do not provide ongoing guidance for teachers as they attempt to learn and change their practices. Killion and Harrison (2006, p. 8) concur that, 'traditional professional development usually occurs away from the schools site, separate from classroom contexts and challenges in which teachers are expected to apply what they have learned, and often without the necessary support to facilitate transfer of learning'; this sentiment is similarly echoed by Moss (2008) and Ostermeier *et al.* (2010). In sum, scholars agree and research supports that when used in isolation, the prevalent 'event' model of professional development for traditional face-to-face classroom teachers is not effective in changing classroom practice (for example, Joyce and Showers 1995).

Leading the way in responding to the plethora of research documenting the ineffectiveness of one-time workshop professional development experiences, the premier professional development association in the United States, Learning

Forward (formerly the National Staff Development Council), has made it the organization's mission to insist that 'every educator engages in effective professional learning every day so every student achieves' (Learning Forward 2012). According to Learning Forward, high-quality professional development emphasizes systematic, planned, intentional and regularly scheduled efforts to embed teacher learning within teachers' daily lives.

Beyond the United States, others are making strides to transform professional development for teachers. In New Zealand's In-Service Teacher Education Project (INSTEP), facilitators worked with teachers to implement and understand important features of professional learning to be attended to in mentoring teachers (Davey and Ham 2010). Throughout the course of their two-year study, they noted that relevant professional learning is tied to teachers' practice and everyday realities of the classroom, allows teachers to be the subjects of their own inquiry, is manageable, is sustainable over time, balances support and challenge and empowers teachers. In a professional learning collaboration between Japan and South Africa, educators engaged in lesson study as a way to study their own work, reflect upon their learning and collaborate with others in order to critically examine and continue to develop their own professional identities, knowledge and practice (Ono *et al.* 2011). In Israel, teachers engaged in self-regulated learning as professional development, which provided teachers with opportunities to be active participants in their own learning, ultimately helping them to demonstrate increased content and pedagogical knowledge (Kramarski and Revach 2009). Together, the principles set forth by Learning Forward (2012), INSTEP (Davey and Ham 2010), lesson study (Ono *et al.* 2011) and self-regulated learning (Kramarski and Revach 2009) illustrate a concept known as job-embedded professional development (Yendol-Hoppey and Dana 2010).

The concept of job-embedded professional development is consonant with what research suggests effective professional development that goes beyond the one-time workshop looks like (Little and McLaughlin 1993, Garet *et al.* 2001, Lee 2005). Specifically, Desimone (2009, p. 183) suggests that, 'a research consensus [exists] on the main features of professional development that have been associated with changes in knowledge, practice, and, to a lesser extent, student achievement'. These core features of effective professional development include active learning, coherence, duration and collective participation, all of which can be actualized through a professional development programme of action research (Yendol-Hoppey and Dana 2010, Dana *et al.* 2011).

Action research involves teachers spiralling through a series of steps that include the posing of questions, the collection and analysis of data, making informed changes to practice and sharing findings with others (Dana and Yendol-Hoppey 2009). Action research has proven to be a powerful tool for teacher professional development (Zeichner 2003), an important vehicle to raise teachers' voices in educational reform (Meyers and Rust 2003) and a mechanism for expanding the knowledge base for teaching (Cochran-Smith and Lytle 1993, 2009).

Because the process of action research has proven both its utility and value in traditional face-to-face classroom contexts, the process also holds great promise for the world of virtual schooling. Just as face-to-face classroom teachers utilize action research to gain better understandings of themselves and their classroom practice, virtual teachers may be able to utilize this process to gain deeper insights into their roles as virtual school educators and the promise of online teaching and learning.

Action research also holds potential for the virtual schooling context as it continues to develop as a field of research, policy and practice (Blomeyer 2002, Cavanaugh *et al.* 2004). According to Ferdig *et al.* (2009, p. 480), 'the field is currently lacking a strong body of research knowledge that investigates the elements of pedagogy and practice used by successful virtual school educators'. Hence, virtual school teacher engagement in action research not only can serve as a mechanism for personal professional development but can also add to the developing knowledge about virtual school teaching practices.

The promise action research holds for informing online teaching and learning led the first state-wide Internet-based public high school in the United States, referred to here as ABC Virtual School (a pseudonym), to pilot a year-long programme of action research for their employees. ABC Virtual School is a state-led virtual school that employs nearly 1400 people (70% full-time teachers, 22% non-instructional support staff or administrators and 8% adjunct or part-time instructors). The number of students attending ABC Virtual School is approaching 100,000, with enrolments expected to increase to 500,000 in the next five to seven years. The majority of students enrolled (64%) attend public school and use the virtual school to take courses not available in their home district or for credit recovery (i.e. to earn credits not initially earned due to failing or not completing courses). Nearly one-third of students attending ABC Virtual School are home-schooled and a small percentage comes from private schools.

As a research team at a local university with expertise in action research with face-to-face school contexts as well as educational technology and online learning pedagogy, we were invited to design a pilot programme for ABC Virtual School. We aligned our programme design efforts with the literature on action research, emphasizing support for virtual educators through five critical junctures in the process (detailed below). Thirty participants took part in the professional learning pilot programme. Throughout the various junctures of the pilot, the technologies utilized included interactive Elluminate sessions (i.e. a synchronous conferencing system), email contact, interaction on Schoology (i.e. a learning management system designed to support communication and collaboration), telephone conferencing and an online tool called Action Research for Technology Integration (ARTI), developed by one of the authors to provide a place to collect action research work.

Programme description: virtual teacher action research

Adapted from the work on classroom-based practitioner research, virtual teacher action research refers to the process of a virtual school teacher engaging in systematic, intentional study of his/her own practice and taking action for change based on what she/he learns as a result of action research. There are five critical junctures in the action research process: learning what action research is; defining and refining a personal question for exploration; creating a plan for action research; collecting and analysing data; and sharing what was learned with others (Dana and Yendol-Hoppey 2008). The 30 virtual school educators in this case study attended a series of interactive Elluminate sessions, delivered in October and November of the 2010/11 school year, designed to support them through the first three critical junctures named above (Dana *et al.* 2012).

Following the three Elluminate sessions, the 30 action researchers were divided into four small coaching groups consisting of six to eight teachers each, with each member of our research team serving as the personal action research coach for one group. Through frequent email contact and interaction on Schoology as well as telephone conferencing, we structured professional conversation among group members in which the virtual teachers provided feedback for each other at different times in the action research process. Small group synchronous sessions and asynchronous discussion activities were held at three times: as the teachers developed a plan for their research; as they collected and analysed data; and as they prepared to share their completed research with other virtual school teachers.

These small group sessions and activities were structured by the use of protocols, defined as 'a script or series of timed steps for how a conversation among teachers on a chosen topic will develop' (Dana and Yendol-Hoppey 2008, p. 7). The use of protocols to guide the virtual school teachers' asynchronous and synchronous conversation during the action research professional development programme is illustrated by a description of small group data analysis work using Schoology and telephone conferencing.

To begin, prior to a small group synchronous telephone conference meeting, each virtual school teacher researcher was asked to complete the steps summarized in Table 1 to create a post.

Prior to the synchronous telephone meeting, the virtual teachers were asked to visit the Schoology site to refamiliarize themselves with their small group members' research as well as to become acquainted with what each teacher researcher had learned so far from their data by reading each other's postings. Furthermore, each teacher researcher was asked to have the Schoology site opened on their computer during the synchronous telephone conference meeting so they could glance at each person's written summary of the action research as they provided feedback to one another.

At the synchronous meeting, one by one, each small group member had the opportunity to share his/her research and receive feedback on the data analysis process by following an adaptation of the Data Analysis Protocol (see Dana and Yendol-Hoppey 2008). Utilizing this protocol, each virtual school educator briefly

Table 1. Schoology post directions.

Step One	Gather collected data in one place and organize
Step Two	Read through entire dataset once to get a sense of the dataset as a whole
Step Three	Read through entire dataset a second time, keeping track of what you noticed by making a list entitled 'Action Research – What I'm Noticing'
Step Four	Complete the following open-ended sentences:

- The issue/tension/dilemma/problem/interest that led me to my action research was:

- Therefore, the purpose of my action research was to:

- My wondering was:

- I collected data by:

- So far, three discoveries I've made by reading through my data are:
  (1)
  (2)
  (3)

Step Four	Post open-ended sentence completion responses on Schoology site

reminded the group of his/her action research, summarizing and referring to the post on the Schoology site. The members of the group then took turns asking probing questions of the presenter in order to gain a deeper understanding of the action research. The questioning was then followed by a discussion among the remainder of the group, sharing thoughts and suggestions about the presenter's action research, while the presenter remained silent, listening and taking notes. The presenter then reflected on what he or she heard in the group discussion, sharing with the group anything particularly resonant.

Following the synchronous small group data-analysis telephone meetings, each researcher finished up data collection and analysis and utilized ARTI, developed by Dawson *et al.* (2009), to capture their action research work. ARTI provided a space for the virtual teachers to upload their individual research to a larger database, which we could later use to analyse salient features of the action research process pertinent to these teachers' learning. Finally, all action researchers presented their work to other virtual school teachers via Elluminate sessions held in May.

Homeschool Homeroom: an example of action research conducted during the programme

The action research process as enacted by virtual school teachers is exemplified by the research of two participants in this study. During our introductory session, two virtual school teachers began conversing about a similar dilemma – the rising population of new home-schooled students who were enrolling in their biology classes and the unique needs this population brought with them to the virtual school context. In addition to the needs associated with learning the biology content, these students were also in need of developing an understanding of the virtual school's policies and procedures as well as developing the skills and work habits necessary to be successful independent online learners. To address this dilemma, these two teachers posed the following question: 'What strategies can we incorporate as virtual school teachers to support new home school students?'

To gain insights into this question, the teachers recreated the concept of 'homeroom' from the traditional face-to-face environment in the online context. To understand how their virtual homeroom was working, the teachers collected data in three ways: conducting a survey of students to understand their perceptions of homeroom participation and the meaning a virtual homeroom held for their learning and motivation to complete their coursework; monitoring the attendance of students at homeroom over time; and saving artefacts and email/text communication produced by students related to homeroom activity.

As a result of analysing their data, these teachers were happy to report that once new home-schooled students attended a virtual homeroom session, they returned to future sessions and, despite virtual homeroom being an optional activity, offered apologies when they were unable to attend. For example, one student wrote the following message:

> Hi, sorry about missing homeroom. I had an eye exam. I will be there next week though. So sorry again.

In addition, these virtual school teacher researchers reported that while their home-school students enjoyed the social/fun side of Homeschool Homeroom best, they also found homeroom a valuable place to learn about virtual school procedures and the biology course in which they were enrolled. In fact, over 66% of the students reported that they attended Homeschool Homeroom to get to know other home-school students while 33% reported that they attended either to learn more about virtual school procedures or to learn more about the biology course. This led the virtual school teacher researchers to focus on the ways they might capitalize more on the value their students reported in getting to know other home-school students and the ways they might incorporate these students' need for social interaction into course learning activities.

In sum, the results of this study led to the following actions: the refinement of Homeschool Homeroom to make it more effective in meeting the needs of students; and the fine-tuning of some biology course learning activities to heighten students' interactions with one another. Sharing their research with colleagues in their virtual school enabled other virtual school professionals to reflect on the ways they were and were not meeting the unique needs of their home-school student population, and created a rich space for dialogue around the action the virtual school might take as a whole to create special programmes and experiences that target the learning needs of not just home-school students but also other special virtual school student populations.

Research methodology

As the 30 virtual teachers engaged in action research, we documented and studied programme development and the ways these teachers were experiencing the process of action research; in essence, modelling the process of action research for the virtual school teachers we coached in the process. We were guided by the following research question: 'In what ways do virtual school teachers describe their experience with professional development when it is framed as a year-long collaborative action research endeavour supported by the use of various synchronous and asynchronous technology tools?'

Our research into the experience of action research for virtual school teachers is interpretive (Erickson 1986) in nature and draws on case-study methodology (Stake 1995) informed by a phenomenological lens (Denzin and Lincoln 1994). Phenomenologists seek to understand the lived experience and meaning the experience holds for research participants (Patton 2002). In this case, we were interested in documenting and determining the essence of the experience of engaging in action research as a mechanism for the professional development of virtual school teachers and the ways these virtual school teachers made sense of both their prior professional development experiences and engagement in action research as a professional development model enacted in virtual schools.

Data sources

To understand and document the experience of virtual teachers' engagement in action research as a form of professional development, the primary source of data for this study was individual interviews. As we were both the facilitators of this professional development experience as well as the researchers, we conducted these participant interviews after the professional development programme was over and our relationship as these teachers' action research coaches had ended. In addition, to assure that the participants' responses were not influenced by their prior relationship with us as their action research coaches, a team member that had not served as the participant's action research coach conducted the individual interviews.

We utilized a modified version of Seidman's (1991) phenomenological interviewing process. When utilizing Seidman's phenomenological interviewing process, researchers frame interview questions for the participants with three separate emphases, each building upon the other. The first emphasis is on the life-history of each participant in relation to the topic, putting participants' experiences in context. The second emphasis is on the details of experiences with the topic of study. The third and final emphasis is reflection, in which participants synthesize, articulate and make meaning of their experiences. Through questions that focused on these three emphases, participants were asked to describe what it was like to conduct action research as virtual school teachers.

Although Seidman suggests conducting three separate interviews with a few individuals, Seidman's three prescribed interviews were condensed into one interview due to the relatively large number of participants in the study, but the questions posed during the interview focused on the three key areas: Focused Life History (how they came to be virtual school teachers and prior experiences they had with professional development); Details of Experience (how they experienced professional development in their virtual school as well as the action research professional development programme); and Meaning of Experience (the ways they understood the totality of all professional development experiences). Sixteen participants agreed to participate in a one-hour interview. The interviews were tape-recorded and transcribed verbatim.

In addition to the interviews, secondary sources of data for this study include artefacts that were produced for use in or during each Elluminate session, field notes taken during synchronous sessions and the action researchers' final presentations in May, and all entries made by the action researchers in the ARTI system, encompassing 25 studies completed by 30 virtual school teachers.

Complete copies of all data were made for each member of the research team. Data analysis consisted of many readings and re-readings of the dataset by each member of the research team individually, during which time analysts independently coded the data for themes and patterns. The research team met frequently, creating the space for multiple analysts to share, discuss and debate patterns emerging in initial review of interview transcripts and other forms of data (Marshall and Rossman 2010). Through these discussions, findings emerged related to these virtual teachers' experiences with action research as professional development. Analyst and source triangulation, as well as member checking, enhanced the trustworthiness and credibility of this study (Patton 2002).

Findings

The participants' professional development experiences could be described in three distinct categories: memories of traditional face-to-face school professional development experiences; professional development offerings by the virtual school; and action research as professional development.

Memories of traditional face-to-face school professional development experiences

In general, participants described their memories of traditional face-to-face school professional development experiences as very traditional. Professional development was an event referred to as 'in-service', held on a day when students did not come to school, and was often disconnected from the daily work of the classroom teacher. In alignment with research on teacher professional development (Desimone 2009), the participants found little meaning and value in professional development when it was structured in this way:

> [The district I worked for] would provide in-services on how you use Excel, how you use the new standards, classroom management, different things like that ... My face-to-face classroom teaching professional development experiences were pretty much the same thing every year, boring me out of my skull. They really were.

> I can recall being at the traditional school and having a training that was eight hours with a one-hour break in between. You would leave and that would be the end of it.

In addition to in-service workshop days, some participants described another similar common professional development venue – a menu of classes offered by the districts in which they were employed. Similar to the in-service full-day workshops, these professional development opportunities were removed from practice, as teachers had to ask permission from their administrators to leave their classrooms to attend a class and, if permission was granted, the administrator needed to hire a substitute teacher for the day to cover the participating teachers' instructional duties. One participant explained:

> The school district where I worked [before coming to the virtual school] offered classes but I had to seek them out ... You'd have to go and look for the list of classes that were offered by the district and then you'd have to ask permission to attend and sometimes you were given permission and sometimes you weren't ... It was up to the administration and if the administration didn't feel that we needed it or if they weren't willing to spare us for a day or a half a day for professional development, they just didn't let us go ... It wasn't necessarily that they didn't want you to learn, it was more, 'Well we can't give you up because we're shorthanded; we need you here or we prefer that you stay in the classroom instead of go and take this training.'

While the participants found some value in select traditional face-to-face school professional development experiences they had, by and large they were concerned by the lack of follow up to in-service days and district-offered class experiences:

> With this type of professional development, you attend a class, you listen to what they're saying, you do a few activities and then you're kind of done and whether you decide to carry on that skill or not, what you've learned is up to you.

> If I took a standard face-to-face school professional development it was more of a lecture type. Occasionally it would be hands-on but it was learn this new practice, go back to your classroom, try it, and there was very little follow-up and there certainly was not a lot of time spent looking at what results we had and how we implemented what we learned ... I would say about fifty percent of the time it was useful and fifty percent of the time I felt like I was just filling a seat.

One participant went on to share that the pedagogy employed during in-service workshops and district classes was not conducive to adult learning:

> I tend to find that a lot of times in professional development we do everything in those courses that we tell teachers not to do in their classrooms. So you know we sit

people down in a room for eight hours straight and we talk at them. If we did that in the traditional school it would be mayhem and we'd probably lose our job because that is not what you're supposed to do. Yet we expect adults to just sit and take it and learn and I don't think that that is realistic, you know? ... That just killed me.

Overall, the participants in this study did not describe the majority of their traditional face-to-face school professional development experiences positively, with their descriptions confirming practice documented in the professional development literature as ineffective.

The result of one-day workshops with little to no follow-up that often employed poor pedagogy for adult learners was summed up by one participant in the following way:

I'm thinking back to being in a traditional face-to-face school for as long as I have and seeing things forced upon teachers instead of having them buy into it.

Once becoming employed by the virtual school, however, participants describe a shift in experience:

In the traditional school I found that most of the professional development was something you were told to do. There really wasn't very much offered at my school so it didn't necessarily pertain to me or my teaching which was very frustrating ... I found that there's a lot more opportunities to actually help me be a better teacher at [the virtual school where I work].

Professional development offerings by the virtual school

The participants in this study described excellent choice and easy accessibility to numerous professional development opportunities in their virtual environment:

When it came to ABC Virtual School, it was easier to access professional development; there were just a lot of choices available. Signing up was easy. I was able to choose different sessions, usually hour-long online sessions, about a variety of topics that would help me on the job.

These one-hour online sessions were praised by numerous participants for their relevance to the virtual school teacher and contrasted with the traditional in-service professional development day experience by their length, accessibility and choice for participation:

We call them sessions – they're just one-hour sessions on technology, and, you know, different things that you can use in your [teaching]. They are similar to an [in-service] event but shorter, more accessible, more focused on meeting the learning needs of virtual teachers. More choice, not forced.

In contrast to their face-to-face school in-service day counterpart, 'sessions' were also praised by participants for the flexibility they afforded:

You know it's not like I have to leave [a classroom]; it's very flexible because everything we do here is flexible because we all work online. So like today, for example, I'm working from home ... The flexibility [is great]. And you might have a conflict like you have a session and a phone conference with a student scheduled at the same time, but usually we offer sessions so many times, the same session three or four times, that if you can't make it to one then you make it to the next session or because we record the sessions because they're online on Elluminate, you can watch the recording and still participate by doing the follow-up activities or whatever it might be.

In addition to sessions, a noteworthy professional development experience shared by the virtual school was teacher-to-teacher online gatherings, where different virtual school educators would share pedagogical approaches to online instruction:

We have [these gatherings] where you could learn from other teachers' best practices, which I think that right there in and of itself makes it easier because if someone is already putting something into practice and they're showing you that they're reaping positive rewards from it, then it makes it feel like, 'Oh, I can do that, too.' You can talk to that person and relate to them: 'How much time did this take? How much time do we need to set aside to start doing this? Is this something we can jump right in with? Can you help me?' You know when you're able to collaborate with a teacher who's already doing something, I think that opens up a lot of doors for teachers.

The teacher-to-teacher sessions helped the participants feel that the craft knowledge they possessed associated with online teaching and learning was valued by the organization and valuable to others. This sense of being valued and being valuable was also enforced by this virtual school organization's willingness to send its teachers to conferences:

Because I live in a rural county, a traditional school is more likely to encourage people to go see whoever is around. Whereas ABC Virtual School will say we like this; we'll send you to it even if it means travel. I've also noticed that with virtual school too, if there's something that interests me I can approach my instructional leader with it for approval as opposed to not even having a shot in the traditional school environment.

In contrast to face-to-face school professional development memories, virtual school professional development was more relevant and immediate to the needs of these educators, and more aligned with what the literature says about critical aspects necessary for the learning of teachers – choice, flexibility and collaboration (see Desimone 2009). These attributes of professional learning led these virtual school teachers to feel valued and respected, a clear difference from the ways these teachers recollected feeling about the professional development they experienced from their face-to-face teaching days.

Yet, the participants were quick to point out that while better than their prior experiences, the professional development they had experienced as virtual teachers was not perfect:

Professional development in the virtual school is better I think because it is virtual, so by nature, it is a lot more hands-on. When you are learning technology you have your computer in front of you; you are using it instantly. When it came to the sessions, though, what I found was in many ways, it was the same thing. You were getting just a virtual lecture as opposed to a face-to-face lecture … What I still see in both environments is there is a lot of information given and we struggle with implementation and evaluating the impact on students' achievement. We struggle with it in the virtual environment. I'd love to say we've got it figured out here but we don't.

Hence, the virtual educators in this study still yearned for professional development opportunities beyond all they had experienced as both face-to-face and online teachers. These feelings were reflected in the reasoning participants gave for their decision to join the pilot action research programme at ABC Virtual School:

> I thought this is something new, this is something different and I like reflection so I was really on board to try something different for a change and have it be professional development as well … We've become automated and I think a process like action research encourages us to step outside of our comfort zone or step outside of our habits and make us do something different.

In the English language, 'pushing the envelope' is a common phrase often utilized to denote the attempt to exceed the current level of performance, to innovate and/or to push current and commonly accepted boundaries. Engaging in action research as professional development 'pushed the envelope' on these virtual school teachers' professional development experiences, extending and deepening those aspects of professional development that were better in the virtual environment in productive and meaningful ways.

Pushing the envelope: action research as professional development

The first notable way that action research pushed the envelope on virtual teacher professional development was the duration of the professional development endeavour:

> Foremost, [engaging in action research] was more comprehensive. It took longer and spanned a longer amount of time. A lot of times with professional learning it's one or two days. You go, you learn it, you take it back, it's done … Because this was over many months, I would say it was quite advanced in its scope.

While this finding is not surprising, since Desimone (2009) denotes duration as one of the critical features of a successful professional development programme, it is ironic. Recall that these virtual school teachers praised the shortened one-hour length of the online sessions available at their virtual school over their memories of the eight-hour in-service from their traditional face-to-face teaching days, equating shorter professional development with better professional development. Yet, through their participation in a sustained, long-term programme of action research that unfolded over many months, they realized the limitations of short-term professional development previously experienced. Where once they valued a short one-hour session over an eight-hour day, engagement in action research offered a whole new way to think in relationship to professional development:

> It was the first time I've actually sat back and watched what I was doing, and that was a really interesting experience and I loved it. It's easy to sign up for a session and take notes and hear about great things you could try, but to be able to sit back and kind of observe yourself and see exactly what's working for you and what isn't working for you … I know all the theory and so forth, but really and truly, how am I carrying it out with my students? … That was professional development like I've never experienced it before.

The second notable way that action research pushed the envelope on virtual teacher professional development was in relationship to the notion of choice:

[Action research] was much more diverse in the things that we were learning about and the things that we were discussing and it was much more meaningful for the participants than in general one person teaching to the masses provides.

Recall that these virtual school teachers praised the great variety and easy accessibility to different sessions one could attend online over their memories of a single, same-day, same-time in-service attended by all during their traditional face-to-face teaching days, equating choice with the provision of a 'menu' of workshops. However, because the process of action research begins by defining an individual research question, engagement in action research gave the concept of 'choice' a whole new meaning:

With action research, we kind of drove the bus. We picked an item of our own choosing rather than someone saying, 'Oh, we're going to have a seminar today.' That we got to pick our focus – that was definitely different.

Choice was now defined as picking a focus for one's research as opposed to picking an event to attend. An important benefit of this re-definition of choice in professional development was that action research made professional development self-directed, rather than other-directed:

I could pick the direction and find something that interested me and that I had a question about … It was something I chose to do and something I questioned and not something that someone told me I had to do or told me I should look into. That was really great, just me having a choice to know what to do.

Because teachers' research questions emerge from their daily work with students, action research as professional development is directly related to the learning and achievement of students – a second benefit of the individualized and self-directed nature of the action research experience:

With traditional professional development you go, you sit, you listen and then you're supposed to take something from it whereas [with action research] you go and you implement and then you review it and you analyse data and you use your thinking and you're not just sitting there getting information; you're actually processing it and putting it back out there to figure out what's best for your students.

This benefit extends through teachers' sharing of their action research with one another:

I think on a daily basis we're trying to figure out how we can teach the students in this online environment. I think through action research, whether it's another teacher doing it and sharing their results, or if it's you doing it and sharing your results, it's a great way to find out what's working and what's not working with our students.

The third notable way in which action research pushed the envelope on virtual teacher professional development was in relationship to the notion of learning from other teachers. Recall that these virtual school teachers praised the teacher-to-teacher sessions offered by their virtual school where colleagues would share pedagogical approaches to online instruction, equating teacher collaboration with the swapping of good online teaching ideas. While the action research sharing sessions that occurred at the culmination of the action research professional development programme were praised in a similar fashion, sharing between teachers was experienced in new ways through action research.

As a part of the action research professional development programme, small groups of virtual teachers and their action research coach interacted on Schoology and conferenced by telephone to provide feedback for each other as they developed a plan for action research, collected and analysed data and prepared to share their completed research with other virtual school educators. Learning from other teachers became more than just swapping ideas for good online pedagogy and swapping the results of an action research journey:

> [Through action research], we were able to be more involved in feedback to one another and also we probably gained a higher level of insight from our peers because we interacted on the Schoology site and over the phone. It wasn't just emailing feedback where you write, 'Good job; let me know if you have any questions.' That's kind of really one-dimensional. Action research forced us to be more, just more purposeful and to have a deeper level of communication with one another.

The sharing and collaborative conversation that was done through action research also pushed the envelope of the sharing and collaborative conversation that was done in the virtual school teacher-to-teacher sessions, in that the action research conversations were data-driven. Participants discussed how collecting and analysing data as a part of the action research process afforded them greater credibility as they shared their online teaching practice with their colleagues:

> I had concrete data so it wouldn't just be, 'Well, this is what I think.'

> [Prior to action research], what I suspected and what my gut told me was all I had, but I couldn't verify it … I didn't have anything to back up what I was doing, other than my gut.

Data-driven conversations were seen as invaluable to the future of ABC Virtual School:

> We see a need for [data-driven work] in ABC Virtual School. It's really important. We know we do great work but we need data to back up what we're doing and action research is a great way for people to look at their practices and use data to improve.

Discussion

As the field of virtual teacher professional development is still in its infancy (Dede *et al.* 2009), an important finding from this study is that it is imperative not to settle for the *status quo* of virtual teacher professional development even if it appears on the surface to be better than what virtual teachers traditionally have experienced in their past traditional face-to-face school contexts. This study indicated that while virtual school professional development experiences may be in greater alignment with what is known about teacher professional development, a programme of virtual school action research can push the envelope on the ways teachers engage as learners and collaborators with one another to better understand and enact the online teaching phenomenon.

Furthermore, an examination of the ways virtual school teachers experience action research as professional development affirms the critical role action research can play in the continuous learning of all teachers, regardless of the traditional face-to-face or the newer online context. Through examining action research through the eyes of virtual teachers, it becomes clear that action research is greatly aligned with much of what we know about professional development and adult learning theory (see, for example, Knowles 1973, Brookfield 1992, Mezirow and Associates 2000).

First, adults have ownership in and of their learning. No longer is professional development something done to them by others. Rather, they control and participate in their learning. Second, engagement in action research is differentiated. Not all teachers are learning the same thing in the same way at the same time. Rather, action research establishes a path for learning to emerge for each educator based on his/her needs and current context. Third, in large part, action research is self-directed as teachers take initiative and responsibility for the design and implementation of the action research cycle – selecting a question that is relevant and meaningful to explore, managing data collection to gain insights into the question and assessing their own learning through data analysis. Fourth, since professionals begin the process of action research by articulating a burning question that emerges from a felt difficulty or dilemma in practice, by definition and design, the process of action research enables teachers' learning to be immediate and relevant to their lives and work as educators and to the learning of their students. Fifth, action research is collaborative. Teachers discuss and critically reflect on practice together through meaningful and structured dialogue, collectively constructing knowledge about practice. Finally, the process of action research is active and engaging. Rather than passively participating in a 'sit and get' workshop, action research 'turns traditional professional development on its head' (Check 1997, p. 6).

Implications

This study has focused on the experiences of virtual school teachers who participated in a year-long collaborative action research endeavour and provides clear implications for other virtual schools and virtual school educators interested in merging action research and online professional learning as evidenced from the discussion above.

Merging action research and online professional learning may also have implications for the professional development of all teachers, including those in traditional face-to-face environments learning to teach online. The technology provides a means by which professional development can transform from 'fragmented, intellectually superficial seminars' (Borko 2004, p. 4) to rich, ongoing, job-embedded experiences (Yendol-Hoppey and Dana 2010). However, technology does not cause this transformation. Deliberate use of technology to support effective professional development practices is essential.

The Community of Inquiry model (Garrison *et al.* 2001) provides a concise framework to guide development of online professional learning for teachers. The framework outlines three components of an online educational experience: social presence; cognitive presence; and teaching presence. Social presence refers to the ability of learners within an online educational experience to present themselves and view others as important individuals in the learning process. Cognitive presence refers to the way the online learning is structured to support sustained meaning-making through communication. Teaching presence refers to the facilitator's ability to design and direct cognitive and social processes within the online educational experience. While neither a thorough review of the Community of Inquiry framework nor a review of technologies to support it is within the scope of this article, an important implication of this work is that design of online professional learning must involve individuals with expertise in technology use, online teaching and learning, professional development and content. The technology, in and of itself, is neutral and can support various professional development strategies depending on how it is used.

Future research

This study focused on the experiences of virtual school teachers who participated in a year-long collaborative action research endeavour. Our current research is studying the benefits, challenges and limitations of this programme. Preliminary results show that time and communication with supervisors about the action research professional development were challenges, while benefits included personal growth, professional learning and positive changes in their professional practices and opportunities to learn from and share with others. Current research is also exploring the nature of the action research questions asked by the virtual school educators and how they took ownership of these questions to modify their practice.

Additional research might look at a similar online learning experience for face-to-face classroom teachers learning to teach online or at the effect, if any, of having prior knowledge of action research during such an online learning experience. Research might also explore the facilitators and constraints of using different technology tools to support the online learning experience or of different designs to support the action research process.

Conclusions

This study demonstrates that the merger of action research and online professional learning can have positive results for virtual school teachers. Teachers reported that the professional learning experience positively changed their practices and motivated them professionally. In addition, the online professional learning experience supported core features of effective professional development, including active learning, coherence, duration and collective participation (Yendol-Hoppey and Dana 2010, Dana *et al.* 2011). While there is much still to learn about promising practices for virtual school teacher growth and development (and for the growth and development of face-to-face classroom teachers learning to teach online), the results of this study indicate one sure thing: to turn traditional professional development on its head (Check 1997) through the merger of action research and online professional learning is a positive direction for the future of the field.

References

Altrichter, H. and Posch, P., 2010. Reflective development and developmental research: is there a future for action research as a research strategy for German-speaking countries? *Educational action research*, 18 (1), 57–71.

Appana, S., 2008. A review of benefits and limitations of online learning in the context of the student, the instructor and the tenured faculty. *International journal on e-learning*, 7 (1), 5–22.

Bai, Y., 2009. Action research localization in China: three cases. *Educational action research*, 17 (1), 143–154.

Barbour, M., *et al.*, 2011. *Online and blended learning: a survey of policy and practice of K–12 schools around the world*. Vienna, VA: iNACOL.

Barnett, M., 2002. Issues and trends concerning electronic networking technologies for teacher professional development: a critical review of the literature. *Paper presented at the annual meeting of the American Educational Research Association*, 1–5 April, New Orleans, LA.

Blomeyer, R., 2002. *Online learning for K–12 students: what do we know now?* Naperville, IL: North Central Regional Educational Laboratory.

Borko, H., 2004. Professional development and teacher learning: mapping the terrain. *Educational researcher*, 33 (8), 3–15.

Brookfield, S., 1992. Developing criteria for formal theory building in adult education. *Adult education quarterly*, 42 (2), 79–93.

Cavanaugh, C., *et al.*, 2004. *The effects of distance education on K–12 student outcomes: a meta-analysis*. Naperville, IL: Learning Point Associates.

Cavanaugh, C., Barbour, M., and Clark, T., 2009. Research and practice in K–12 online learning: a review of open access literature. *The international review of research in open and distance learning*, 10 (1), 1–22.

Check, J., 1997. Teacher research as powerful professional development. *Harvard education letter*, 13 (3), 6–8.

Cochran-Smith, M. and Lytle, S.L., 1993. *Inside/outside: teacher research and knowledge*. New York: Teachers College Press.

Cochran-Smith, M. and Lytle, S.L., 1999. Relationships of knowledge and practice: teacher learning in communities. *Review of research in education*, 24, 249–305.

Cochran-Smith, M. and Lytle, S., 2009. *Inquiry as stance: practitioner research for the next generation*. New York: Teachers College Press.

Dabner, N., Davis, N., and Zaka, P., 2012. Authentic project-based design of professional development for teachers studying online and blended teaching. *Contemporary issues in technology and teacher education*, 12 (1), 71–114.

Dana, N.F., *et al.*, 2012. Virtual educator inquiry: design and implementation of a year-long programme to mentor virtual educators in the action research process. *In*: K. Kennedy and L. Archambault, eds. *Supporting educators in K–12 online learning environments*. Vienna, VA: iNACOL, 115–129.

Dana, N.F., Thomas, C., and Boynton, S., 2011. *Inquiry: a districtwide approach to staff and student learning*. Thousand Oaks, CA: Corwin Press.

Dana, N.F. and Yendol-Hoppey, D., 2008. *The reflective educator's guide to professional development: coaching inquiry-oriented learning communities*. Thousand Oaks, CA: Corwin Press.

Dana, N.F. and Yendol-Hoppey, D., 2009. *The reflective educator's guide to classroom research: learning to teach and teaching to learn through practitioner inquiry*. 2nd ed. Thousand Oaks, CA: Corwin Press.

Davey, R. and Ham, V., 2010. 'It's all about paying attention!' … but to what? The '6 Ms' of mentoring the professional learning of teacher educators. *Professional development in education*, 36 (1–2), 229–244.

Dawley, L., Rice, K., and Hink, G., 2010. *Going virtual! 2010: the status of professional development and unique needs of K-12 online teachers* [online]. Report published by the International Association for K–12 Online Learning. Available from: http://edtech. boisestate.edu/goingvirtual/goingvirtual.htm [Accessed 2 November 2012].

Dawson, K., Cavanaugh, C., and Ritzhaupt, A., 2009. *The evolution of ARTI: an online tool to promote classroom-based technology outcomes via teacher inquiry.* Paper presented at the Society for Technology and Teacher Education (SITE) annual meeting, 2–6 March, Charleston, SC.

Dede, C., 2006. *Online professional development for teachers: emerging models and methods*. Harvard, MA: Harvard Education Press.

Dede, C., *et al.*, 2009. A research agenda for online teacher professional development. *Journal of teacher education*, 60 (1), 8–19.

Denzin, N.K. and Lincoln, Y.S., 1994. *Handbook of qualitative research*. Thousand Oaks, CA: Sage.

Desimone, L.M., 2009. Improving impact studies of teachers' professional development: toward better conceptualization and measures. *Educational researcher*, 38 (3), 181–199.

Erickson, F., 1986. Qualitative methods in research on teaching. *In*: M.C. Wittrock, ed. *Handbook of research on teaching*. 3rd ed. New York: Macmillan, 119–161.

Ferdig, R.E., *et al.*, 2009. Virtual schooling standards and best practices for teacher education. *Journal of technology and teacher education*, 17 (4), 479–503.

Garet, M.S., *et al.*, 2001. What makes professional development effective? Results from a national sample of teachers. *American educational research journal*, 38 (4), 915–945.

Garrison, D.R., Anderson, T., and Archer, W., 2001. Critical thinking, cognitive presence, and computer conferencing in distance education. *American journal of distance education*, 15 (1), 7–23.

Greenwood, J., Te Aika, L.H., and Davis, N.E., 2011. Creating Virtual Marae: an examination of how digital technologies have been adopted by Maori in Aotearoa New Zealand. *In*: P.R. Leigh, ed. *International explorations of technology equity and the digital divide: critical, historical and social perspectives*. Charlotte, NC: Information Age Press, 58–79.

Halai, N., 2011. How teachers become action researchers in Pakistan: emerging patterns from a qualitative metasynthesis. *Educational action research*, 19 (2), 201–214.

Hardy, I. and Rönnerman, K., 2011. The value and valuing of continuing professional development: current dilemmas, future directions and the case for action research. *Cambridge journal of education*, 41 (4), 461–472.

International Association for K–12 Online Learning, 2012. *Fast facts about K–12 online learning*. Vienna, VA: iNACOL.

Joyce, B.R. and Showers, B., 1995. *Student achievement through staff development*. White Plains, NY: Longman.

Killion, J. and Harrison, C., 2006. *Taking the lead: new roles for teachers and school-based coaches*. Oxford, OH: National Staff Development Council.

Killion, J. and Pinata, R., 2011. *Recalibrating professional development for teacher success*. Education Week Webinar.

Knowles, M., 1973. *The adult learner: a neglected species*. Houston, TX: Gulf Publishing.

Kramarski, B. and Revach, T., 2009. The challenge of self-regulated learning in mathematics teachers' professional training. *Educational studies in mathematics*, 72 (3), 379–399.

Learning Forward, 2012. Available from: http://www.learningforward.org/index.cfm [Accessed January 2012].

Lee, H.J., 2005. Developing a professional development programme model based on teachers' needs. *The professional educator*, 27 (1), 39–49.

Lieberman, A., 1995. Practices that support teacher development: transforming conceptions of professional learning. *Phi delta kappan*, 76 (8), 591–596.

Little, J.W. and McLaughlin, M.W., eds., 1993. *Teachers' work: individuals, colleagues, and contexts*. New York: Teachers College Press.

Lipowski, K., *et al.*, 2011. Expert views on the implementation of teacher professional development in European countries. *Professional development in education*, 37 (5), 685–700.

López-Pastor, V.M., Monjas, R., and Manrique, J.C., 2011. Fifteen years of action research as professional development: seeking more collaborative, useful and democratic systems for teachers. *Educational action research*, 19 (2), 153–170.

Marshall, C. and Rossman, G.B., 2010. *Designing qualitative research*. 5th ed. Thousand Oaks, CA: Sage.

Meyers, E. and Rust, F., 2003. *Taking action with teacher research*. Portsmouth, NH: Heinemann.

Mezirow, J. and Associates, 2000. *Learning as transformation: critical perspectives on a theory in progress*. San Francisco, CA: Jossey Bass.

Moss, J., 2008. Leading professional development in an Australian secondary school through school–university partnerships. *Asia-Pacific journal of teacher education*, 36 (4), 345–357.

Ono, Y., *et al.*, 2011. Reflections on a mutual journey of discovery and growth based on a Japanese–South African collaboration. *Professional development in education*, 37 (3), 335–352.

Opfer, V.D. and Pedder, D., 2011. The lost promise of teacher professional development in England. *European journal of teacher education*, 34 (1), 3–24.

Ostermeier, C., Prenzel, M., and Duit, R., 2010. Improving science and mathematics instruction: the SINUS project as an example for reform as teacher professional development. *International journal of science education*, 32 (3), 303–327.

Patton, M.Q., 2002. *Qualitative research and evaluation methods*. Thousand Oaks, CA: Sage.

Rice, K., 2009. Priorities in K–12 distance education: a Delphi study examining multiple perspectives on policy, practice, and research. *Educational technology & society*, 12 (3), 163–177.

Seidman, I.E., 1991. *Interviewing as qualitative research: a guide for researchers in education and the social sciences*. New York: Teachers College Press.

Somekh, B. and Zeichner, K., 2009. Action research for educational reform: remodeling action research theories and practices in local contexts. *Educational action research*, 17 (1), 5–21.

Sparks, D. and Hirsh, S., 1997. *A new vision for staff development*. Alexandria, VA: Association for Supervision and Curriculum Development.

Spicer, D.E. and Dede, C., 2006. Collaborative design of online professional development: building the Milwaukee Professional Support Portal. *Journal technology and teacher education*, 14 (4), 679–699.

Stake, R., 1995. *The art of case study research*. Thousand Oaks, CA: Sage.

Sugrue, C., 2011. Irish teachers' experiences of professional development: performative or transformative learning? *Professional development in education*, 37 (5), 793–815.

Toomey, R., *et al.*, 2005. Lifelong learning and the reform of the teaching practicum in Australia. *Asia-Pacific journal of teacher education*, 33 (1), 23–34.

Yendol-Hoppey, D. and Dana, N.F., 2010. *Powerful professional development: building expertise within the four walls of your school*. Thousand Oaks, CA: Corwin Press.

Zeichner, K., 2003. Teacher research as professional development for P–12 educators in the USA. *Educational action research*, 11 (2), 301–326.

Framing pre-service teachers' professional learning using Web2.0 tools: positioning pre-service teachers as agents of cultural and technological change

Warren Kidd

Cass School of Education and Communities, University of East London, London, UK

This article addresses key issues in pre-service teachers' professional learning. The argument explores pre-service teachers' learning and practice, which is both informed by technology and which uses technologically enhanced practices in classrooms as learning and teaching strategies. The article is contextualized by current international debates regarding technicist and rational post-modern professional learning cultures, performativity and national standards. The article positions pre-service teachers as potential agents of change for schools.

Introduction

This article explores the view that pre-service teachers need to learn about, learn how to use and learn through technology. This argument is contextualized within debates about teaching as a craft practice. The contribution this article makes to these debates is in positioning craft practice as a counter-point to neo-liberal agendas and discourses in education; it reworks notions of 'craft' to explore the links between pre-service teacher learning and the use of technology and emerging digital literacies of new teachers. To do so, it positions pre-service teachers as potential change agents for schools. The argument is that Web2.0 tools provide essential opportunities for exploration and innovation for teachers – these tools provide opportunities for a craft pedagogy. By Web2.0 tools, we refer to the second formation of the Web – the 'social web':

> The second incarnation of the Web (Web 2.0) has been called the 'social Web', because, in contrast to Web 1.0, its content can be more easily generated and published by users, and the collective intelligence of users encourages more democratic use. (Kamel Boulos and Wheeler 2007, 2)

In this Web2.0 world, schools and colleges, it is argued, should now be focusing their attention on educating highly technologically skilled generations of children and young people for the fast-changing world of the twenty-first century (Chapman *et al.* 2010). In recent political discourses, children and young people are constructed as 'expert' users of new technologies, hyper-media and the Internet, and education is positioned as a major way of achieving technology-driven knowledge economies globally (Selwyn 2009). Teachers are sometimes positioned as 'catching-up', disenfranchised and disempowered as their learners become repositioned by these discourses (Prensky 2001a, 2001b). Buttressing this claim are those who suggest that the 'digital native' debate in which all young people are seen as 'immersed experts' is under-evidenced (Helsper and Eynon 2010) and that so-called 'digital natives' are less informed about new technologies than policy rhetoric might suggest (Wan 2012).

A different set of policy discourses, also demanding educational change, sees teacher education as an important lever for improving the quality of schooling. Reflecting this, there are ongoing international debates about how best to develop effective and appropriate modes of education and training, particularly in pre-service provision, which is seen as the fastest and most effective route to achieve change (see, *inter alia*, Barber and Mourshed 2007, Cochran-Smith 2011, MacBeath 2012).

Bringing together these two calls for educational change, it would seem clear that provision for pre-service teachers' learning should be centred on encouraging the deployment of new technologies as a key part of their future pedagogy. Yet analysis of current research in this article indicates that many pre-service programmes do not so much embed the use of new technologies as central to student learning; rather, they adopt an 'add on' strategy in which a limited range of applications are included in essentially traditional modes of provision. In the university-based elements of many programmes, there is limited use of new technologies (Biasutti and El-Deghaidy 2012), much of it following the 'add on' strategy, with implications then for how we might construct in the future teacher education pedagogies. For example, nearly all universities now use Managed Learning Environments to disseminate information and communicate with students. Demonstrations by teacher educators of Information and Communication Technology (ICT) applications used in schools, such as interactive white boards, as part of seminars or lectures provide further examples of the 'add on' strategy in use.

When pre-service teachers go out into schools for practicum, the classroom contexts in which they could learn to teach with and through new technologies may also be limited. This is because, despite the rise of hyper-media and the ubiquity of the digital world, technology is still an 'outsider' in many schools and within many teachers' pedagogy. Current research (Chapman *et al.* 2010, Conole and Alevizou 2010), for example, suggests that it is only a minority of teachers in the United Kingdom who are developing approaches to practice that consider the full possibilities technology might afford. Existing provision for pre-service teachers to learn with new technologies – across both universities and schools – may be described then as 'patchy', at best.

This evidence poses implications, then, for the pedagogy and practice of teacher educators to support the developing digital literacy and technology tool use of pre-service teachers within their own pedagogy (Sadaf *et al.* 2012). It is possible to argue that the very innovation on which e-learning and technology-enabled pedagogy are based *requires* a rethink and restructuring of professional learning cultures and structural forces: 'Innovation requires vision, sensitivity, playfulness and energy at grass roots level and changes to structures and regulatory frameworks at the organizational and policy levels' (Somekh 2007, p. 2). The argument here is that the adoption of technology practices within craft practice can lead to sustained and important reflective and reflexive work (Lee 2006). Thus, the choices teachers make and the creativity and imagination behind meaningful technology-supported pedagogic practice can lead to a re-think of identity constructions and identity roles. Equally, pre-service teachers' technologically rich craft practices can work as a change agent for the schools they train and are employed in (Price and Valli 2005, Donnison 2007).

This article positions this 're-think' as a two-fold issue: it has implications for the development of the *craft practice* of teachers; it is an issue of training and *professional learning*. It is, then, a question of how teachers perceive their role and their practice in an ever-changing world. Perhaps because of the limited provision for ICT in many schools beyond the use of Managed Learning Environments and interactive white boards, the integration of new technologies in pre-service education is not extensively researched, although there is a growing body of studies. This article aims to make a contribution to this important and developing research base by offering an analysis of that available research. It then makes a further contribution to the field by drawing on the analysis to explore the usefulness of emergent technologies and digital literacy for pre-service students' professional learning. The paper argues that the globalized rise of powerful Web2.0 tools allows for significant developments in teacher education curricula and pedagogy that resonate with the development of pre-service teachers' pedagogic 'craft' practices. These arguments are framed within the context of international debates on the nature of teachers' professional learning and the roles played by technology in education. The article also draws upon the ideas of Giddens (1984, 1991) and Somekh (2007), locating debates on technology and craft practice within a broadly structurational context.

Drawing on this body of literature, pre-service teacher education (and practice) is understood here as 'a way of being' (Feldman 1997, p. 757). It is not so much that teachers 'do' teaching, but rather that they are 'being' a teacher. Thus, practice and professional roles that underpin such practice offer a contextualized location for their professional understandings and also their identity constructions. Campbell (2003) speaks of the increased need of 'ethical agency' for teacher professionalism as a means to move forward ethical knowledge in practice. Teachers need to recognize that e-cultures are often entrenched and resistant, but that individual practice can make a difference (Somekh 2007). There is a need to conceive teachers as knowledgeable agents able to create opportunities for change in craft practice (Giddens 1984), while also recognizing that technology offers a site for innovation. To move e-learning craft practices forward, we need to support teachers' professional development to learn about, learn how and learn through new technological forms. The potential for innovation in craft practice exists (Beetham and Sharpe 2007) despite its slow expansion (Laudrillard 2007, Beetham *et al.* 2009). This positions craft work as also identity work (Grimmett and MacKinnon 1992, Pollard 2010) and frames technological innovation as a site for 'artistic connoisseurship' (Eisner 1979), essential for professional learning and professional learning cultures.

To explore the constructions of teaching as a craft, including the use of technology-enabled learning for innovation, this article draws on the writings of Sennett (2008) on 'craftsmanship' [*sic*] and the insights of Somekh (2007) on innovation in teaching and teachers' learning. Bringing together these claims, this article poses the following questions: How can pre-service teachers be supported to engage more meaningfully with new and emerging mobile and e-learning technologies? How can teachers learn *about*, learn *how* to use and learn *through* new technologies? (How) can pre-service teachers act as agents of change within schools? Firstly the article will explore the cultural context of professional learning into which pre-service teachers enter. Secondly, in the light of this context, the article will explore a paradox within e-learning – the apparent fruitfulness of the tools and learning opportunities and yet the sparse 'regular' normative practice – before then going on to look at the implications technologically rich practice and professional learning might have for teacher education. Finally, these debates about pre-service teachers' learning through and about technology will be contextualized within debates regarding craft practice and the performativity (Lyotard 1979) of global policy contexts.

Rationalism and performativity: the context of teachers' learning

Craft practice and technologically rich learning and teaching as craft practice do not operate in a context devoid from structural forces and the pressures of policy rhetoric and discourses. If pre-service teachers are potential change agents, then what is the context of professional learning that they enter? There is growing international interest across the world for in-service teachers' professional learning (Whitty 2000, Brown *et al.* 2001) and the role of leadership cultures (Hargreaves and Goodson 2006, Mulford 2008) in developing this. International analyses of in-service professional learning often adopt a socio-cultural perspective (see, for example, Hersey *et al.* 2001, Scott 2010) when discussing how leadership and learning cultures might move professional learning forward, sometimes framed as the 'enabling school' (Arthur *et al.* 2010). Within this, there are numerous criticisms of neo-liberal discourses and practices that seek to 'improve' schools and teaching through surveillance cultures and performativity (Ball 2003). These are widely seen as forces to control professionals and professionalism, as the increase of Weberian rationalization (Arthur *et al.* 2010, drawing on Weber 1968) or as the onward spread of the 'McDonaldization' of teaching (Ritzer 2000). Others (see Hargreaves and Fullan 1998) see that where teacher professional learning is described as 'rational' or 'technical', approaches and responses to institutional need fail to understand the chaotic and unique nature of educational institutions and the learning communities within them.

The inherent contradiction between the prescription of uniform national 'standards' of teaching competence monitored through the mechanisms of bio-politics (Foucault 1975) and surveillance (Ball 2003) and the 'complex' nature of effective pedagogies is associated with the rise of globalization and a 'standardization' process that undermines professional autonomy (Menter *et al.* 2006). For others (Whitehead 2005, Nielsen and Pedersen 2011), these changes are part of the wider forces of change associated with the post-modern condition and the reallocation of knowledge (Hargreaves 1994, 2000): the rise of local, flexible, pragmatic modes of production that reshape the role education and training have for a workforce working within a global economy.

As Lyotard originally notes:

> … these technological transformations can be expected to have a considerable impact on knowledge … [and are] already changing the way in which learning is acquired, classified, made available and exploited. (1979, p. 125)

Following Giddens' (1984, 1991) structurational view of a reflexive modernity, global and national change and reform – shaped by the forces of globalization – have local consequences for the formation of teachers' lives and selves. This point is echoed by Somekh (2007) about applying the twin forces of structure and agency to the implementation of technology craft practice in the classroom and teachers' learning of these practices.

Drawing together these lenses, we can think about how e-learning and technologically rich professional learning are situated within craft practice. In this view, craft knowledge is more than understanding – it is more than just 'rules of practice'. Rather, it is '… all the complex, largely tacit knowledge that informs the contextualized professional judgments made by individual teachers in their everyday practice' (Hagger and McIntyre 2006, p. 34). Equally, for McNamara and Deforges (1978) the craft knowledge of teachers needs to be seen as both valuable and valid: it needs to be seen to offer academic theorizing a different perspective – a counter, rooted in practice itself. Indeed, as Hagger and McIntyre suggest, the role of craft knowledge within the professional practice of teachers is to do much more than simply allow them to 'get by': craft knowledge offers deep knowledge located within the emerging identities of practitioners as they enter teaching and learning communities. In the discussion that follows this metaphor is applied to pre-service teachers' learning about and through technological innovation.

Learning *about*, learning *how* and learning *through* technology

The origins of the term 'e-learning' and its potential significance for education can be traced to a speech by Jay Cross in 1998, where he states:

> We thought we could take the instructors out of the learning process and let workers gobble up self-paced (i.e., 'don't expect help from us') lessons on their own. We were wrong. First-generation e-learning was a flop. (Cited in Mason and Rennie 2006, p. xiv)

From its origins, then, the development of the potential role for technology in education is one of training and the appropriateness of professional learning. Within political discourse, the importance of technology in education is often linked to a rhetoric of lifelong learning and the need for global skills competition (Mason and Rennie 2006). Yet the research paints a different picture – one of huge pedagogic potentiality, tempered and contradicted by a lack of meaningful development and slow expansion (Beetham and Sharpe 2007, Laudrillard 2007, Beetham *et al.* 2009, Chapman *et al.* 2010). Despite the rapid rise of hyper-media and the ubiquity of the digital world and globalized forces, technology is still an 'outsider' in many schools and within much teacher craft practice. This may, in part, be because technology '… sits uncomfortably with teachers' professional judgments' (Watson 2001, p. 251). e-Learning is sometimes described as a 'rapid' and intensified phenomenon (O'Neill *et al.* 2004). But, in counterpoint to this idea, the Learning Literacies for a Digital Age project (Beetham *et al.* 2009) identifies that education is still required to perform a 'shift' in its engagement with technologies for learning. If teachers are asked to add these tools to their craft practice, then this is an issue to be addressed in both pre-service and in-service learning. It may take time for teachers to be able to engage with technology because of issues of culture and infrastructure (Beetham and Sharpe 2007), and because '... despite the ubiquity of technology in the business world, no clear role has emerged in education' (Watson 2001, p. 251). It requires a re-think of pedagogy as well as the construction of cultures of professional learning and professional practice that are collective, communal and about 'doing and making' and playing with tools (Mayes and de Freitas 2007, Gauntlett 2011). Yet, creative, imaginative and appropriate technology-enhanced pedagogy will only be possible if teachers are, '... empowered to develop localized or novel responses to socio-technical change – including developing new approaches to curriculum, to assessment, to the work force and governance, as well as to pedagogy' (Attwell and Hughes 2010, p. 65).

Pre-service teachers and digital-rich pedagogies – are they agents for change?

The use of digital tools, emerging technologies and social media within teacher education has implications for the skills and pedagogy of teacher educators: 'New techniques of pedagogy have to be practiced, and new skills learnt' (ESCalate 2006, p. 12). Yet, as Magliaro and Ezeife (2007) note, '... equipment and connectivity do not guarantee successful or productive use'. In reviewing the nature of e-learning practices, Roblyer (2003) has noted how teachers' views on and attitudes to new educational technologies have an impact on how they use them (within craft practice) and, in turn, how future technology may be implemented. This is also true for the teacher educators who train them. Magliaro and Ezeife (2007) suggest that, '... many in-service (currently teaching) and pre-service (currently in training) teachers believe that they are not adequately trained and often are not given appropriate tools to implement educational technology in their classrooms'. Kolb (2008) notes that many teachers need to undergo a 'belief change' at the heart of their practice with ICT – their learning needs to incorporate technology practices into their 'pedagogic filters'. For Kolb, to best support pre-service teachers, teacher education pedagogies need to model 'everyday pedagogical technological strategies'. Equally:

> ... the challenge of integrating technology into the classroom has provided a motivation for teacher educators to engage in continual improvements in the curriculum to equip teachers who could cope with the multifarious demands in the school environment. (Teo *et al.* 2008, p. 170)

Given that '... teachers act as change agents for technology integration in schools' (Teo *et al.* 2008, p. 163), then pre-service teachers as they enter the profession might be better positioned to act as change agents. Here we find, '... implications for teacher educators who must find ways of encouraging pre-service teachers to evaluate current practices surrounding digital technology in the classroom' (Burnett 2009, p. 127). And yet as Burnett (2009) also notes, studies of the professional development of teachers indicate that alignment to existing practice within institutions – fitting into the norm – is often a source of reward for teachers. Thus, acting as a change agent is both a risky and potentially alienating professional location. In addition, the use of technology-rich pedagogies to support pre-service teachers' learning does not necessarily mean such practices can comfortably translate into their own teaching craft (Karagiorgi and Charalambous 2006). Furthermore, research indicates that simplistic arguments that younger pre-service teachers are more likely to be 'digital natives' and more likely to have their own extensive personal digital literacies are exaggerated (Bennett *et al.* 2008, Chapman *et al.* 2010).

Cowan *et al.* (2011) speak in the United Kingdom of the 'limited transition' to teacher education pedagogies adopting Web2.0 practices. They suggest there is:

> ... little evidence of familiarity with the additional pedagogical tools available; tutors have not been trained in use of the modern online pedagogies; the technology is constantly ahead of the pedagogy; and there is a lack of availability of professional development activities to model effective use of new technologies. (Cowan *et al.* 2011)

Within the Australian higher education context, Saltmarsh and Sutherland-Smith (2010) note that many suspicions surround digital pedagogies amongst teacher educators, often framing movement to digital tools as 'cost-cutting'. Thus, '... the transition [to technology-rich pedagogies] for many teacher educators is fraught with tensions and contradictions' (Saltmarsh and Sutherland-Smith 2010, p. 15). Burnett (2011) notes that asking pre-service teachers to adopt pedagogic practices that might tap into existing digital literacies is fraught with multiple and contradictory tensions around legitimacy, risk and appropriateness of such tools and practices.

Ubiquitous learning? Understanding technology-enabled professional learning

Drawing on the above research and borrowing an insight from Ljubojevic and Laurillard (2011), it is possible to develop a highly situated understanding of how and why teachers learn things. These writers suggest that for teachers to be able to accommodate a new tool or technique into their (craft) practice, they need first to understand why the approach would be useful. This tacit understanding of techniques comes from a step-by-step approach to professional learning that structures in each new idea, in turn, allowing for meaning-making around why it is useful in and for practice. When applied to teacher professional learning with and through technology, this presents a contradiction: on the one hand, it is recognized that Web2.0 tools and hyper-media offer something of 'interest' – something stimulating, due to their qualities of playfulness and interaction (Kamel Boulos and Wheelert 2007). Yet, at the same time, ICT is often resistant to being incorporated into learning and teaching practices (Somekh 2007), as previously explored. Equally, many school institutions are reluctant, culturally, to enact change where technology is concerned. Drawing upon the work of Bidwell (2001), technology is in this case an example of an innovation that has '...failed to penetrate the forces of socio-cultural reproduction built into the institutional structures of schools' (Somekh 2007, p. 114). This makes 'bringing technology in' to resistant cultures difficult, but still innovation is possible. To explain this *en passé* – the inability for radical change through the introduction of technology in education and the incomparability of school structures and the resistance of teacher cultures – Somekh (2007) adopts the structuration theory of Giddens (1984, 1991), who suggests that: '... according to the notion of the duality of structure, the structural properties of social systems are both medium and outcome of the practices they recursively organize' (Giddens 1984, p. 25). This makes placing technology-enabled learning at the heart of initial teacher education more important. Yet it is argued that there is an uneasy fit – 'the nature of the Internet is inherently individualistic, anarchic, exploratory and disruptive' (Somekh 2007, p. 115). The cultures of resistance to technology-enabled learning are experienced by many pre-service teachers as they boundary-cross into new educational institutions to develop their craft practice. What does this mean for teacher education, and in particular for the professional learning of pre-service teachers? First, it is important to recognize the ability for resistance within institutions to cultural change, yet to also understand that, in the complex dynamic between structures and agency, individuals can change both the nature of the practices they act out and the frame within which they act (Giddens 1984). This interplay between structure and agency positions pre-service teachers as both objects of the forces of institutional normative patterns and routines, yet also potential catalysts for institutional change.

To support the use of technology-enabled learning within initial teacher education, Somekh asserts a model of innovative change based upon five key characteristics (drawn from Somekh 2007):

(1) Messiness – recognize that those who manage change need to see change as messy and as often 'non-mechanical' in nature.
(2) Individuals have the power to bring about change – drawing once more upon the insights of a theoretical frame based upon Giddens' (1984) 'structurational sociology', Somekh suggests that we need to encourage professional learning cultures that are positive about the role of the teacher and practitioner to bring about change.
(3) The importance of partnership in professional learning – the notion that 'shared meanings' bring practitioners together and can have a massive impact upon practice.
(4) Teacher continuing professional development needs to be central to implementing innovation.
(5) Theory and practice need to be further integrated.

In the final section, drawing these arguments together, this article offers insights on the continued usefulness of the craft metaphor when evaluating the role technological-enabled learning can play in schools and in teachers' professional lives.

Craft and technology – a framework for creativity in teachers' learning?

Discourses which suggest that teaching and learning to teach are crafts are gaining strength in current education policy in England. For example, John Hayes, Minister for Business and Skills in 2010, suggested that: '… the instinctive value we feel for craft must be reflected by our education system … this is, this must be the age of the craftsman' (Hayes 2010). And, Michael Gove, the UK Secretary of State for Education at the time of writing, stated that: '… teaching is a craft and it is best learnt as an apprentice observing a master craftsman or woman' (Gove 2010, cited in Derrick 2011, p. 8). These discourses of craft and the policy rhetoric surrounding them contribute to shaping current performativity cultures in education. They also shape university and school responses to the ways in which pre-service and in-service learning opportunities are created, and lend legitimacy to those professional learning practices. Yet the discourses found in current government policy are not the only interpretation of teaching as craft. Craft may also be used as a metaphor that allows recognition of the importance of complex practice and significant professional identity change. This is especially true for learning using technology, as argued above.

The craft metaphor has within it notions of '… the desire to do a job well for its own sake' (Sennett 2008, p. 9); a notion of quality potentially undermined by performativity cultures. As Sennett suggests, although:

> … craftsmanship can reward an individual with a sense of pride in work, this reward is not simple. The craftsman often faces conflicting objective standards of excellence; the desire to do something well for its own sake can be impaired by competitive pressure. (2008, p. 9)

In adding a moral or ethical dimension to the craft metaphor, craft practice itself can be positioned as a question of identity:

> The key to craft, and to teaching, I suggest, is not so much what the craft worker or teacher specifically does (though this is of course very important), but the kind of person they are. The first task of craft workers, from this perspective, is to produce themselves. (Derrick 2011, p. 8)

Again, Sennett (2008) poses a useful question – where has the craftsman [*sic*] gone? Here, 'craft' does not have the derogatory connotation associated with some of the literature (see, for example, Scheffler 1960), but rather it is deeply interwoven into human nature itself as the desire to do a job with skill and pride. The modern meaning of this term as something antiquated and often involving simple forms of labour is rejected. Instead, Sennett offers a view of professionals using tools and developing expertise while taking pleasure in a 'job well done'. These arguments also apply to pre-service and in-service teachers learning about and learning through technology. The craft metaphor is again useful here. Seeing technology-enabled pedagogy practice as a craft-choice, and, in turn, seeing choices around teachers' craft practices and pedagogies as an issue of identity, draws upon the notion of 'artistic connoisseurship' (Eisner 1979):

> Through reflection teachers apply the process of artistic connoisseurship to their own practice to judge its worth, and over time deepen their level of understanding of the quality and productive power of their interactions with students. Innovations in pedagogy and learning disturb the continuity of this process, bringing with them, usually from outside, a vision that challenges the teacher to change. (Somekh 2007, p. 2)

Conclusion

Much of the literature on developing and creating e-learning practice – where little might already exist – takes a position embedded in management and leadership practice that frames expanding e-learning as a question of leadership for change and in creating sustained e-cultures (Harris 2009, Gauntlett 2011). The argument in this body of work suggests that e-learning needs cultural change and cultural development for it to be embedded in institutional practices and individual teachers' craft responses (Tomlinson 2001, Stoll and Temperley 2009, Zhang and Brundrett 2010). Webb and Cox (2004) have suggested there is an important need for further teacher professional development and professional learning since technology changes the teacher role, making it more 'complex'. As Sennett notes:

> ... getting better at using tools comes to us, in part, when the tools challenge us ... in both creation and repair, the challenge can be met by adapting the form of a tool, or improvising with it as it is, using it in ways it was not meant for. (2008, p. 194)

Technology-enabled learning can be conceived as a vehicle through, and a site of, potential innovation and change in craft practice. If incorporated into teacher education pedagogy, this is something that would privilege pre-service teachers as offering a distinctly different craft pedagogy to those who might already work in cultures resistant to change, with performativity cultures stifling creativity:

> ... currently in the UK, despite an ambitious programme of investment by government in ICT resources, infrastructure and teacher training, there is no evidence of change of the radical kind observable in the commercial world. It is almost certainly because the structures, rules of behaviour and division of labour (roles) in schools are rooted in long-standing traditions and authority structures, that the potential for ICT to have a significant impact on learning has not so far been realized. (Somekh 2007, p. 155)

This is as true for teachers' craft practice as it is for their own learning. Through this argument, we have positioned professional learning through and about technology as itself contributing to craft practice.

The implications for this article are that teachers and teacher educators need to consider both what teachers do and who teachers come to see themselves as, if pre-service teachers are to effect change in cultural practice. Drawing upon earlier research by Brown and McIntyre (1993), Hagger and McIntyre suggest that there exists a '... rich and expert professional craft knowledge' (2006, p. 79) within teaching as a social practice. In this view, craft knowledge has three fundamental features: it is embedded within practice (and is 'everyday'); it is common across all practitioners; and yet individual teachers-as-craft-persons can nonetheless '... draw on an individual repertoire of craft knowledge for appropriate use in each specific situation' (Hagger and McIntyre 2006, p. 34). Thus, professional craft knowledge has relational and hermeneutic elements – it comes from socialization into a community of practice (Lave and Wenger 1991) and as a result enables the practitioner to know one's self. It also has, as a form of professional knowledge, claims of both an ontology and an epistemology: it allows practitioners to both know *about* and know *of* social practice.

Technology is both a means, a vehicle, through which learning about and learning how to change are achieved and also a pedagogic craft practice, a site, upon which change can manifest, with pre-service teachers acting as potential agents of such change.

References

Arthur, L., *et al.*, 2010. School culture and postgraduate professional development: delineating the 'enabling school'. *Professional development in education*, 36 (3), 471–489.

Attwell, G. and Hughes, J., 2010. Pedagogic approaches to using technology for learning [online]. Available from: http://webarchive.nationalarchives.gov.uk/20110414152025/http://www.lluk.org/wp-content/uploads/2011/01/Pedagogical-appraches-for-using-technology-literature-review-january-11-FINAL.pdf [Accessed 10 October 2012].

Ball, S.J., 2003. The teacher's soul and the terrors of performativity. *Journal of education policy*, 18 (2), 215–228.

Barber, M. and Mourshed, M., 2007. *How the world's best-performing school systems come out on top*. London: McKinsey and Company.

Beetham, H., McGill, L., and Littlejohn, A., 2009. Thriving in the 21st century: learning literacies for the digital age (LLiDA project) [online]. Available from: http://www.jisc.ac.uk/media/documents/projects/llidareportjune2009.pdf [Accessed 31 January 2013].

Beetham, H. and Sharpe, R., eds., 2007. *Rethinking pedagogy for a digital age. Designing and delivering e-learning*. London: Routledge.

Bennett, S., Maton, K., and Kervin, L., 2008. The 'digital natives' debate: a critical review of the evidence. *British journal of educational technology*, 39 (5), 775–786.

Biasutti, M. and El-Deghaidy, H., 2012. Using wiki in teacher education: impact on knowledge management processes and student satisfaction. *Computers and education*, 59 (3), 861–872.

Bidwell, C.E., 2001. Analyzing schools as organizations: long-term permanence and short-term change. Extra issue: Current of thought: sociology of education at the dawn of the 21st century. *Sociology of education*, 74, 100–114.

Brown, S., Edmonds, S., and Lee, B., 2001. *Continuing professional development: LEA and school support for teachers*. Slough: NFER.

Brown, S. and McIntyre, D., 1993. *Making sense of teaching*. Maidenhead: Open University Press.

Burnett, C., 2009. Personal digital literacies versus classroom literacies: investigating pre-service teachers' digital lives in and beyond the classroom. *In*: V. Carrington and M. Robinson, eds. *Digital literacies: social learning and classroom practices*. London: Sage, 115–129.

Burnett, C., 2011. Pre-service teachers' digital literacy practices: exploring contingency in identity and digital literacy in and out of educational context. *Language and education*, 25 (5), 433–449.

Campbell, E., 2003. *The ethical teacher*. Buckingham: Open University Press.

Chapman, L., Masters, J., and Pedulla, J., 2010. Do digital divisions still persist in schools? Access to technology and technical skills of teachers in high needs schools in the United States of America. *Journal of education for teaching*, 36 (2), 239–249.

Cochran-Smith, M., 2011. Does learning to teach ever end? *The record*, 22–24.

Conole, G. and Alevizou, P., 2010. *A literature review of the use of Web 2.0 tools in higher education*. York: HEA Academy [online]. Available from: http://www.heacademy.ac.uk/assets/EvidenceNet/ Conole_Alevizou_2010.pdf [Accessed 10 October 2012].

Cowan, P., Neil, P., and Winter, E., 2011. *Face-zine the future: moving to online teaching* [online]. ESCalate. Available from: http://www.leeds.ac.uk/educol/documents/207287.pdf [Accessed 10 October 2012].

Derrick, J., 2011. The craft so long to lerne: exploring craft as a metaphor for teaching. *Adults learning*, 22 (8), 8–11.

Donnison, S. 2007. Digital generation pre-service teachers as change agents: a paradox. *Australian journal of teacher education* [online], 32 (4), article 5. Available from: http://ro.ecu.edu.au/ajte/vol32/iss4/5 [Accessed 1 August 2012].

Eisner, E.E., 1979. *The educational imagination*. London: Macmillan.

ESCalate, 2006. *Case study in e-learning practice: integrating e-learning in Initial Teacher Education* [online]. Available from: http://escalate.ac.uk/2398 [Accessed 1 August 2012].

Feldman, A., 1997. Varieties of wisdom in the practice of teachers. *Teaching and teacher education*, 13 (7), 757–773.

Foucault, M., 1975. *Discipline and punish: the birth of the prison*. New York: Random House.

Gauntlett, D., 2011. *Making is connecting. The social meaning of creativity, from DIY and knitting to YouTube and Web 2.0*. Cambridge: Polity.

Giddens, A., 1984. *The constitution of society: outline of the theory of structuration*. Cambridge: Polity Press.

Giddens, A., 1991. *Modernity and self-identity: self and society in the late modern age*. Cambridge: Polity Press.

Gove, M., 2010. *Speech to the National College for Leadership of Schools 17-06-2010* [online]. Available from: http://www.michaelgove.com/content/national_college_ annual_conference [Accessed 1 August 2012].

Grimmett, P. and MacKinnon, A., 1992. Craft knowledge and the education of teachers. *Review of research in education*, 18 (1), 385–456.

Hagger, H. and McIntyre, D., 2006. *Learning teaching from teachers: realising the potential of school-based teacher education*. Maidenhead: Open University Press.

Hargreaves, A., 1994. *Changing teachers, changing times: teachers' work and culture in the postmodern age*. London: Cassell.

Hargreaves, A., 2000. Four ages of professionalism and professional learning. *Teachers and teaching: history and practice*, 6 (2), 151–182.

Hargreaves, A. and Fullan, M., 1998. *What's worth fighting for in education?* Buckingham: Open University Press.

Hargreaves, A. and Goodson, I., 2006. Educational change over time? The sustainability or nonsustainability of three decades of secondary school change and continuity. *Educational administration quarterly*, 42 (1), 3–41.

Harris, A., 2009. Creative leadership: developing future leaders. *Management in education*, 23 (1), 9–11.

Hayes, J., 2010. *Speech to the Royal Society of Arts 26-10-10* [online]. Available from: http://www.bis.gov.uk/news/speeches/john-hayes-skills-and-their-place [Accessed 18 February 2013].

Helsper, E. and Eynon, R., 2010. Digital natives: where is the evidence? *British educational research journal*, 36 (3), 503–520.

Hersey, P., Blanchard, K.H., and Johnson, D.E., 2001. *Management of organizational behavior: leading human resources*. Upper Saddle River, NJ: Prentice-Hall.

Kamel Boulos, M.N.K. and Wheeler, S., 2007. The emerging Web 2.0 social software: an enabling suite of sociable technologies in health and health care education. *Health information and libraries journal*, 24 (1), 2–23.

Karagiorgi, Y. and Charalambous, K., 2006. ICT in-service training and school practices: in search for the impact. *Journal of education for teaching*, 32 (4), 395–411.

Kolb, L., 2008. Developing everyday technology pedagogy in pre-service teachers, Paper presented at the American Educational Research Association annual meeting, 23–28 March, New York.

Laurillard, D., 2007. Marginalia 48. *In*: G. Conole and M. Oliver, eds. *Contemporary perspectives in e-learning research. Themes, methods and impact on practice*. Abingdon: Routledge, 48.

Lave, J. and Wenger, E., 1991. *Situated learning: legitimate peripheral participation*. Cambridge: Cambridge University Press.

Lee, R., 2006. Using asynchronous discussion to support the reflective thinking of ITE students. *In*: A. Jackson, ed. *Teacher education futures: developing learning and teaching in ITE across the UK. A selection of conference papers presented at St Martin's College, Lancaster 19 May 2006*. Bristol: ESCalate, 5–9.

Ljubojevic, D. and Laurillard, D., 2011. Evaluating learning designs through the formal representation of pedagogical patterns. *In*: C. Kohls and J. Wedekind, eds. *Investigations of e-learning patterns: context factors, problems and solutions*. Hershey, PA: IGI Global, 86–105.

Lyotard, J.-F., 1979. *The postmodern condition: a report on knowledge*. Manchester: Manchester University Press.

MacBeath, J., 2012. *Learning in and out of school: the selected works of John MacBeath*. Abingdon: Routledge.

Magliaro, J. and Ezeife, A.N., 2007. Pre-service teachers' preparedness to integrate computer technology into the curriculum. *Canadian journal of learning and technology* [online], 33 (3). Available from: http://www.cjlt.ca/index.php/cjlt/article/view/163/153 [Accessed 2 August 2012].

Mason, R. and Rennie, F., 2006. *E-learning: the key concepts*. London: Routledge.

Mayes, T. and de Freitas, S., 2007. Learning and e-learning. The role of theory. *In*: H. Beetham and R. Sharpe, eds. *Rethinking pedagogy for a digital age. Designing and delivering e-learning*. London: Routledge, 13–25.

McNamara, D. and Desforges, C., 1978. The social sciences, teacher education and the objectification of craft knowledge. *British journal of teacher education*, 4 (1), 17–36.

Menter, I., Brisard, E., and Smith, I., 2006. Making teachers in Britain: professional knowledge for initial teacher education in England and Scotland.. *Educational philosophy and theory*, 38 (3), 269–286.

Mulford, B., 2008. *The leadership challenge: improving learning in schools.* Camberwell, VIC: Australian Council for Educational Research.

Nielsen, K. and Pedersen, L.T., 2011. Apprenticeship rehabilitated in a postmodern world? *Journal of vocational education and training*, 63 (4), 563–573.

O'Neill, K., Singh, G., and O'Donoghue, J., 2004. Implementing eLearning programmes for higher education: a review of the literature. *Journal of information technology education*, 3, 313–323.

Pollard, A., 2010. *Professionalism and pedagogy: a contemporary opportunity. A commentary by TLRP and GTCE.* London: TLRP.

Prensky, M., 2001a. Digital natives, digital immigrants: part 1. *On the horizon*, 9 (5), 1–6.

Prensky, M., 2001b. Digital natives, digital immigrants part 2: do they really think differently? *On the horizon*, 9 (6), 1–6.

Price, J.N. and Valli, L., 2005. Pre-service teachers becoming agents of change: pedagogical implications for action research. *Journal of teacher education*, 56 (1), 57–72.

Ritzer, G., 2000. *The McDonaldization of society.* Thousand Oaks, CA: Sage.

Roblyer, M., 2003. *Integrating educational technology into teaching.* 3rd ed. Upper Saddle River, NJ: Merrill/Prentice Hall.

Sadaf, A., Newby, T.J., and Ertmer, P.A., 2012. Exploring pre-service teachers' beliefs about using Web 2.0 technologies in K–12 classroom. *Computers and education*, 59 (3), 937–945.

Saltmarsh, S. and Sutherland-Smith, W., 2010. S(t)imulating learning: pedagogy, subjectivity and teacher education in online environments. *London review of education*, 8 (1), 15–24.

Scheffler, I., 1960. *The language of education.* Springfield, IL: Charles C Thomas.

Scott, S., 2010. Pragmatic leadership development in Canada: investigating a mentoring approach. *Professional development in education*, 36 (4), 563–579.

Selwyn, N., 2009. The digital native – myth and reality. Aslib proceedings. *New information perspectives*, 61 (4), 364–379.

Sennett, R., 2008. *The craftsman.* London: Penguin Books.

Somekh, B., 2007. *Pedagogy and learning with ICT: researching the art of innovation.* London: Routledge.

Stoll, L. and Temperley, J., 2009. Creative leadership teams – capacity building and succession planning. *Management in education*, 23 (1), 12–18.

Teo, T., *et al.*, 2008. Beliefs about teaching and uses of technology among pre-service teachers. *Asia-Pacific journal of teacher education*, 36 (2), 163–174.

Tomlinson, H., 2001. Leadership development and e-learning. *Management in education*, 15 (5), 6–10.

Wan, N., 2012. Can we teach digital natives digital literacy? *Computers and education*, 59 (3), 1065–1078.

Watson, D.M., 2001. Pedagogy before technology: re-thinking the relationship between ICT and teaching. *Education and information technologies*, 6 (4), 251–266.

Webb, M. and Cox, M., 2004. A review of pedagogy related to information and communications technology. *Technology, pedagogy and education*, 13 (3), 235–286.

Weber, M., 1968. *Economy and society.* Totowa, NJ: Bedminster.

Whitehead, S., 2005. Performativity culture and the FE professional. *Management in education*, 19 (3), 16–18.

Whitty, G., 2000. Teacher professionalism in new times. *Journal of in-service education*, 26 (2), 281–295.

Zhang, W. and Brundrett, M., 2010. School leaders' perspectives on leadership learning: the case for informal and experiential learning. *Management in education*, 24 (4), 154–158.

National models for continuing professional development: the challenges of twenty-first-century knowledge management

Marilyn Leask[a] and Sarah Younie[b]

[a]Faculty of Education, Sport and Tourism, University of Bedfordshire, Bedford, UK;
[b]Faculty of Humanities, De Montfort University, Leicester, UK

If teacher quality is the most critical factor in improving educational outcomes, then why is so little attention drawn to the knowledge and evidence base available to support teachers in improving the quality of their professional knowledge? This paper draws together findings from a range of sources to propose national models for continuing professional development (CPD). It examines the unacknowledged problem of providing a sustained approach to improving the quality of and access to the evidence base underpinning teachers' CPD. In the twenty-first century, through the use of digital technologies, the research and evidence base underpinning educational practice surely could be made accessible. The quality of the knowledge base and teacher access to this is rarely if ever acknowledged in the discourses about school and system improvement. The lack of access to the latest research is further compounded by the fact that research published in journals is not generally designed around questions teachers want answered. In short, the knowledge that is produced and the management of it within the education sector lack systemic organisation and dissemination. This paper outlines opportunities for low-cost inter-linked national and international e-infrastructures to be developed to support knowledge sharing and building.

Introduction

> Education reform is top of the agenda of almost every country in the world. Yet despite massive increases in spending (last year [in 2006], the world's governments spent $2 trillion on education) and ambitious attempts at reform, the performance of many school systems has barely improved in decades. (Barber and Mourshed 2007, p. 2)

Barber and Mourshed's work, published as the McKinsey Report 'How the World's Best-performing School Systems Come Out on Top', found there was no direct link between the amount of funding and the quality of teaching; rather, their recommendations focus on the importance of the 'right' people becoming teachers. The quality of their professional knowledge is ignored. This paper, in contrast, pays attention to the nature and quality of professional knowledge in addressing the problem of how the quality of teaching might be improved through improving the research and evidence base underpinning educational practice (Davies *et al.* 2000, Hammersley 2002, Cochrane-Smith and Zeichner 2005) and using digital technologies to facilitate teachers' access to a research-informed professional knowledge base. That such an evidence base is necessary to provide a strong foundation for practice is rarely if ever acknowledged in the discourse about school and system improvement. In England under the Labour Government (1997–2010), investments in systematic reviews of the evidence base for policy and practice[1] revealed that much published education research is small-scale, focused either on the impact of government programmes and 'within school' strategies for improvement or on addressing generic issues of classroom pedagogy (e.g. questioning, explaining, grouping and ability). Little substantial research in subject-specific areas was found (Newman *et al.* 2004), yet national assessment systems prioritise assessment of school students' knowledge and skills in subjects. This lack of research-based professional knowledge on subject specialist issues is further compounded by the fact that research published in journals is not generally designed around questions teachers want answered. In short, the knowledge that is produced and the management of it within the education sector are woefully lacking in systemic organisation and coherence.

Using Web 2.0 technologies to reconceptualise forms of continuing professional development for teachers

If those with responsibility for quality of educational provision in a country do not recognise the need for a research-informed knowledge base accessible to teachers, then the opportunity to reconceptualise teachers' continuing professional development (CPD) offered by the widespread availability of Web 2.0 communications and collaboration technologies may be lost. Outside education, use of these e-tools is helping many private and public-sector organisations in the United Kingdom to a situation where knowledge management is developing as a discipline and is providing processes and tools linked with organisational improvement and effectiveness (see, for example, the opportunities identified by Davies *et al.* 2000, Collison and Parcell 2006, Improvement and Development Agency [IDeA] 2006, 2008, 2009). Research from Henley Business School (UK leaders in the field of knowledge management and in implementing such networks for public and private-sector organisations) indicates that such approaches to knowledge management are having an increasing impact on the expectations of staff and are changing ways of working (Henley Knowledge Management Forum 2008a, 2008b).

The international context for knowledge management in education

The OECD, in a 23-country survey, found practice in education sectors to be lagging behind other major sectors:

> ... the task in many countries is to transform traditional models of schooling ... into customised learning systems that identify and develop the talents of all students. This will require the creation of 'knowledge-rich', evidence-based education systems ... in many countries, education is still far from being a knowledge industry in the sense that its own practices are not yet being transformed by knowledge about the efficacy of those practices .... (OECD 2009a, p. 3)

This paper draws on international policy documents and research projects (see, *inter alia*, China Education and Research Network 2000, Department of Education, Science and Training 2005, Ming-yuan 2006, Department of Education, Employment and Workplace Relations 2007, OECD 2007b, 2010, Indian Government National Council for Teacher Education 2010a, 2010b), as well as work the authors have been engaged in internationally (Leask and Younie 2001, 2009a, 2009b, Leask 2012) to propose a knowledge management model for the education sector. Although drawing on international literature, our main intention here is to focus particularly on the United Kingdom where, although there have been major investments in educational research through research councils and specific initiatives, much of the funding has not been directed at keeping teachers up to date with research most relevant to practice.

The UK context

Programmes funded by UK research councils and charities are very competitive and based on the quality of ideas put forward by applicants. Funding is therefore allocated to those who win those bids rather than to systematic building of an evidence base in areas that matter for schooling. Initiatives such as the Applied Educational Research Scheme in Scotland (Taylor *et al.* 2008) and the Economic Social Research Council-funded Teaching and Learning Research Programme (Procter 2007)[2] were not then primarily designed to provide a coherent evidence base for school-based practice. In any case, projects relying on funding from these sources are not sustainable, and when funding ceases the knowledge created is rapidly outdated.

Over the last 20 years an increasingly sophisticated and shared pedagogical language of practice has developed in teaching and teacher education (see, *inter alia*, Capel *et al.* 1994, 2009, 2013, Loughran 2006, Grossman and Turner 2008). In the United Kingdom this development may be linked with the last government's drive for consistency in core aspects of pedagogy through a 'National Strategies' initiative.[3] In addition, the development of information communication technology (ICT) tools for schools, information on the Internet and the increasing sophistication of software monitoring pupil attainment have all played roles in developing a shared professional understanding of what constitutes high-quality teaching.

But evidence from research undertaken in the United Kingdom with teachers and teacher educators (see, *inter alia*, Leask and Younie 2001, 2009a, 2009b) indicates that access to much of this new knowledge is patchy. In national research on ICT tools for future teachers (Leask and Preston 2010), for example, UK teachers requested an e-infrastructure to provide access to validated knowledge and the means for the collaborative creation of new knowledge. This vision went far beyond the current private and unconnected networks supplied by universities, local authorities and schools and the available free software to a national e-infrastructure with open access linking educators nationwide. The communications challenges that educators currently experience online may be compared with the challenges experienced by disparate communities during the early stage of development of the road infrastructure – where only rough tracks connected settlements, where signposts and maps did not exist and where local knowledge passed by word of mouth was needed to navigate around the country. Currently, e-resources supporting knowledge management for the education sector in England are scattered, inaccessible and incoherent, yet potentially they provide a first port of call for teachers who wish to gain more knowledge. Knowledge, however, is dynamic and ever-changing. Static repositories are not therefore the answer; rather, dynamic repositories of knowledge need to be created and continually tested and refreshed. An example of how this is achieved in medicine is provided by the professional review groups developed within the Cochrane Collaboration.[4] This is a longstanding international medical network, based on professional review groups that take responsibility for reviewing systematically the evidence base for particular areas and publishing this regularly online. A range of funding strategies is used to ensure independence.

As with the Cochrane Collaboration, an e-infrastructure for teaching and teacher education would need to be established with guaranteed independence so the provision had professional credibility and could be maintained, regardless of changes in government. This paper emphasises the CPD and pre-service benefits for teachers through the creation of such an e-infrastructure providing signposts, validation of content and networking to support professional collaboration and work dedicated to the development of professional knowledge. Emerging technologies can already support new ways of gathering research data cost-effectively and rapidly (e.g. teachers using Twitter networks to gain advice on problems), and 'crowd sourcing' of views and online polls provide quick and low-cost ways of sharing and testing out ideas.

The Internet has revolutionised knowledge-sharing and knowledge-building across the education profession and there is potential for these ways of working to improve the quality of access to knowledge. A simple education-specific search tool could, for example, be made available through the OECD or the World Bank to facilitate knowledge-sharing internationally. With a few exceptions, information about useful pedagogical tools and about research and evidence to underpin teaching is currently shared informally through multiple networks such as those supported by professional and subject associations. As previously stated, in comparison with health and local government – for example, the previously cited Cochrane Collaboration systematic review groups[5] and what are now the English Local Government Association and Scottish Improvement Services interconnected online communities[6] – the education sector is considerably behind in harnessing the power of technology to support ongoing professional development, knowledge-sharing and evidence-building.

National models for CPD: what provides the knowledge bases?

In societies that want to be internationally competitive in a global context and where the only certainty appears to be that change – of population, of industry, of economies, of weather – will be rapid and unforeseen, the responsiveness to change of the education system and the population may be the most critical factor maintaining the existing standard of living.

With teaching careers potentially spanning more than 40 years as retirement ages are raised, teachers' CPD is clearly essential. We would argue that having a CPD system that reaches every teacher, every year to provide professional learning on issues relevant to their specific practice would be the gold standard to which a country might aspire. A requirement for a teacher to confirm annually that they have undertaken CPD would also seem to have a role to play. CPD 'points systems', coupled with annual registration dependent on the submission of evidence about professional development are common in a number of professions, including law and medicine. This situation in other professions provides leverage to ensure teachers undertake such CPD. But, crucially, these approaches depend on access to high-quality and relevant learning provision. Centrally funded CPD, undertaken in school time, is simply not an option in England because of the costs and numbers of educators involved (over one million in school-based education). Digital technologies clearly have the potential of providing at least part of the answer, particularly if coupled with a clear CPD system, with the characteristics indicated above, which places the onus on the teacher to keep up to date.

An analysis of international education policy documents (see, *inter alia*, OECD 2009a, 2009b, UNESCO 2010a, 2010b) indicates there is an assumption that an up-to-date professional knowledge base to support educators' CPD exists. Much of the literature around effective forms of provision also generally seems to take the professional knowledge base as static and as a given, as we indicated earlier in this article. This presumption is one that we challenge as fallacious and wishful thinking on the part of policy-makers, not least because our research with teacher practitioners indicates otherwise (Leask and Younie 2009b). Two further examples, given below, reiterate this point, since in neither example is mention made of the quality or source of the knowledge underpinning the proposed CPD provision.

Effective CPD – flexible, just in time, responsive to individual needs

In England, research commissioned by the General Teaching Council for England (2006, 2007) identified four key components of effective CPD (see Table 1), but without discussing the knowledge bases for teaching.

The McKinsey Report (Barber and Mourshed 2007, p. 41), discussed earlier, also identified key indicators for effective CPD (see Table 2). Again, the existence of the knowledge base for improvement is largely taken for granted, although there is some acknowledgement of the need for research in the last item.

This guidance on CPD in these two examples of policy therefore leaves largely unaddressed the issues of who are the providers of this flexible, just-in-time and responsive to individual needs CPD and, crucially, how the quality of teacher knowledge is assured.

Table 1. Four key components of effective CPD.

Broader and deeper CPD	Sustained interactions and interventions give more breadth and depth than short or one-off courses …
Teacher influence	The more influence teachers [have] in tailoring CPD to meet their needs – the more likely they are to find it effective …
Awareness of teachers' career needs	Professional development programmes and opportunities should be designed to take account of the needs and priorities of teachers at different stages of their professional lives and careers …
Developing professional learning communities	Schools should … become 'professional learning communities' in which there are opportunities for support staff and non-teaching professionals to learn alongside teachers in CPD and similar activities …

Source: Adapted from General Teaching Council for England (2006, 2007).

Table 2.   Key indicators for effective CPD.

Question	Best in world
What is the total amount of coaching new teachers receive in schools?	>20 weeks
What proportion of each teacher's time is spent on professional development?	10% of working time is used for professional development
Does each teacher have exact knowledge of specific weaknesses in their practice?	Yes, as a result of everyday activities occurring in schools
Can teachers observe and understand better teaching practice in a school setting?	Yes, teachers regularly invite each other into each other's classrooms to observe and coach
Do teachers reflect on and discuss practice?	Yes, through both formal and informal processes in schools
What role do school leaders play in developing effective instructors?	The best coaches and instructors are selected as leaders
How much focused, systematic research is conducted into effective instruction and then fed back into policy and classroom practice?	Research budget equivalent to $50 per student each year focused on improving instruction

Source: Summarised from Barber and Mourshed (2007, p. 41).

The complexity of knowledge required for effective teaching

Another little-discussed area in the literature on CPD is what steps might be taken to ensure that the provision on offer covers the forms of knowledge required for teaching. These include subject content knowledge, general pedagogic knowledge, curriculum knowledge, pedagogical content knowledge, knowledge of learners and their characteristics, knowledge of educational contexts and knowledge of educational ends such as aims, purposes and values (Capel *et al.* 2009, p. 14, adapted from Shulman 1987). These ideas demonstrate the complexity, range and diversity of forms of knowledge a teacher requires. Different approaches to CPD and different forms of research are required, depending on the nature of the knowledge to be developed. Again, this complexity highlights the urgent need for effective knowledge management processes to be developed in the education sector.

While neither the McKinsey Report nor the General Teaching Council for England Report challenge the quality of the 'explicit' knowledge in the published and publically acknowledged knowledge bases underpinning CPD, both do identify networking with peers and experts as a valued and valuable form of learning (General Teaching Council for England 2006, Pickering *et al.* 2007, Barber and Mourshed 2007). In knowledge management terms, sharing knowledge through networks is a way of accessing the 'tacit' as well as explicit knowledge of a community or practitioners (Lave and Wenger 1991, Oakley 2003).

UK local government sector – knowledge management

In local government in the United Kingdom, as part of a national knowledge management strategy for that sector, a national e-infrastructure to support professional networking has been developed to encourage sharing of both 'tacit' and 'explicit' knowledge. Recruitment and retention of local government staff through the provision of a twenty-first-century professional working environment were also drivers behind the establishment of the initiative (IDeA[7] 2006), which in 2012 had over 100,000 members and over 1000 communities.[8] Research undertaken with over 1300 members of the network shows the wide range of professional outcomes from engagement with these online communities (IDeA 2009). Forty-six per cent of members who made use of this resource for more than two years said that their professional practice had been improved as a result of engaging online with colleagues elsewhere. The research also identified the key benefits of using the resource as: saving time; keeping up to date with current thinking and innovations; the sharing of good practice; avoidance of duplication of work; support for developing ideas; and induction to new roles and staff development, as well as relationship-building (IDeA 2009, p. 5). The same association also provides a web-based knowledge repository for the local government sector and a team of staff to keep this updated.

Knowledge management challenges for the education sector

Equivalent provision for the education sector is starting to emerge, including Glow (a national intranet for education) in Scotland, Ultranet in Victoria, Australia and the National College for School Leadership in England. But the range of special-isms in education means that for such networking to be effective, a national and inclusive approach open to all is required to enable users to find and work with people with similar interests. For those leading the education and training of teach-ers, we argue the need for international collaborative networks.

In the United Kingdom the range of government agencies in education has meant that no single agency sees the provision of the required national e-infrastructure as part of their role. Costs are, however, low for an IDeA-type national and internation-ally accessible environment: start-up costs are needed for the initial environment and then low-cost hosting and development costs with a few staff required to manage applications and the help desk and to ensure coherence across the system. Depress-ingly, major national knowledge management initiatives undertaken by numerous education agencies and associations have resulted in a plethora of small networks, with resulting huge management and development costs and lack of sustainability. This is because, as previously discussed, the networks are often linked to time lim-ited projects. The overall result is fragmentation of energies for the sector.

Educators often have multiple interests; for example, a teacher educator may need specialist knowledge in areas such as mathematics, primary education, teacher education and special needs. The current system requires multiple log-ins even where networks exist without any coherent, joined-up 'portal' to access such net-works, but most institutions provide 'locked down' networks that prevent collabora-tion across localities, regions and national and international colleagues.

There are many virtual networks run variously by commercial companies, teachers, academics, local authorities, professional associations, examination boards or universities, but the fragmented nature of what is available and the lack of inter-operability means that the potential of e-networking to improve professional practice is not realised. For example, software called NING is commonly used by teachers, as a Google search demonstrates. At the time of writing there are at least three geography NING online networks in the United Kingdom, which do not link up because of software limitations. In seeking information on geography teaching, then, a teacher wanting access to a good range of resources and networks would have to go separately to the Geographical Association Network and the examination board environments, as well as other more informal geography teaching networks.

Crucial functions identified by teachers (Leask and Preston 2010) as necessary characteristics for an effective online environment are the ability to search for people or projects and the opportunity to move between different communities within the same environment. In the same research, teachers also identified that online environments needed to be networks that enabled them to: find peers interested in similar issues; work online to share ideas, documents and information; collaborate on projects with known colleagues rather than anonymous contributors; and work together with academics, other teachers, local authority staff and policy-makers.

Increasingly, those being recruited to pre-service teacher education courses can be expected to be digitally literate, not only familiar with Web 2.0 Facebook-type environments and networking technologies but aware of the ways in which digital technologies might support high-quality practice. They may also question government expectations that high-quality education will be delivered by teachers, if that same government has not provided the means to harness digital technologies to achieve that quality of practice. Publications from the UK Teaching and Learning Research Programme project (Carmichael and Procter 2006, Procter 2007, Laterza et al. 2007) and Procter's ongoing research with student and newly qualified teachers reveal high levels of expectation that research-based knowledge will be available online. There is also clear dissatisfaction with existing advice in various web spaces that are not research based.

Further examples from other sectors

Reference was made earlier to the Henley Business School Knowledge Management and its work with public and private-sector organisations for whom they provide a knowledge-sharing and knowledge-building network. The IDeA, one of the Henley network members also discussed earlier in this paper, provides examples of five key knowledge management behaviours expected for public-sector staff: finding and using existing knowledge to inform practice; sharing knowledge; creating new knowledge; and managing knowledge (IDeA 2008). Staff members were expected to demonstrate these behaviours in their annual reviews and the same expectation was placed in job descriptions. An expectation such as this, applied across the education sector, could potentially revolutionise practice and relationships between academics and teachers. It could also create an environment where ongoing learning was a natural outcome of engagement in professional activity, which focused on building, reviewing and updating professional knowledge. Figure 1 and the following explanation show how ICT tools might support development of these behaviours in the education sector. The figure also highlights opportunities for improving knowledge management in education to support CPD and updating of staff.

Emerging technologies bring new opportunities and unforeseen challenges. In England, until recently, finding some validated and explicit knowledge for educators via online databases was relatively easy. Funds committed by the government meant that the Education Evidence Portal and the Teacher Training Resource Bank[9] complemented the material on other government agency sites such as the TeacherNet and Qualifications and Curriculum Development Agency websites,[10] with Teachers TV providing complementary video material.[11] With the change in government in

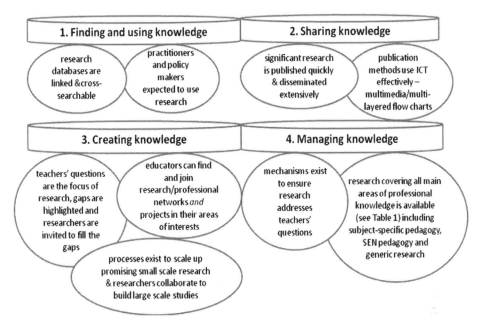

Figure 1. A model for knowledge management provision for national education systems. Source: Leask (2012).

the United Kingdom in May 2010, these sites were decommissioned (with the exception of the Education Evidence Portal, which was not owned by the government). The content was, in theory, to be archived on a UK National Archives website. For technical reasons, however, it is now very difficult to find these resources. Effectively, online resources – which were developed over 13 years and at a cost of £20 million of taxpayers' money – were rendered unusable. Previously, such materials would have been paper-based and copies would have remained in some libraries at least. Clearly, leaving online databases that hold valuable professional knowledge under the control of governments can lead to catastrophic loss of that knowledge. This certainly poses challenges for the future funding and management of databases.

Interesting new developments in the structuring and preservation of knowledge in other sectors may indicate ways to address these challenges. The Map of Medicine Health Guides or flow charts, for example, provide practitioners and patients with ways to access the knowledge they need, in the form they need it.[12] Developed by doctors involved in providing training for new doctors and professional development for their colleagues, the Map of Medicine is run as a commercial enterprise that provides some measure of guarantee of sustainability. The resource provides an alternative way of constructing and communicating knowledge, which is not widely available in education.

Sharing knowledge

How, then, are teachers to share knowledge with peers and researchers? Michael Barber, co-author of the previously discussed McKinsey Report (Barber and

Mourshed 2007), sets out a vision that requires governments to have a new vision for how they might work on using technologies to support whole-system improvement. He states:

> It is not enough for teachers to learn only from within their own schools. The combination of the system improvement and pedagogical knowledge we now have with data and technology places us on the brink of a breakthrough in improving education systems – but as yet not many systems have taken the courageous steps to cross the threshold. (Barber, personal email communication, 2009)

The vision that Barber and the teachers contributing to the Becta ICT Futures research (Leask and Preston 2010) have for an e-communications infrastructure, supporting the education sector to improve, goes beyond what is currently available from any source. It is not difficult to imagine local teacher networks set up to problem-solve in particular areas, using benchmarking data to identify questions and dilemmas and using data to monitor improvements. Such local networks could provide relevant CPD for their members. A national/international e-infrastructure would, however, be needed to support more sustained and wide-ranging levels of communication.

Creating knowledge

As previously stated, the professional knowledge base for teaching is not static, as it needs to evolve with society and educational changes. There are now improved e-communications tools that support collaborative working and which could produce significant improvements in the quality of new knowledge underpinning professional practice and the speed of its dissemination. The introduction of ICTs or digital technologies into educational practice provides a challenging example of the need for new professional knowledge to be produced rapidly. The lack of an infrastructure for sharing this new knowledge has undoubtedly contributed to the patchy implementation of new practice using ICTs in England (Becta 2008, Kitchen *et al.* 2006, Smith *et al.* 2008, Learning Skills Network 2008) with corresponding lack of return on national investment.

Managing knowledge

The expansion of research on neuroscience, much of which has implications for teaching, provides a different example of the challenges of managing and accessing knowledge for educational practice. How are teachers to find out about the recent research that may have implications for their work? In the case of neuroscience, new practice in general pedagogic knowledge and in pedagogic content knowledge has needed to be developed, tested and then disseminated, an initiative in which the OECD took a lead in commissioning research (OECD 2007a). They found that their forums around this topic were heavily used whilst the project was running but, without an international e-infrastructure to support their continuance, these forums ceased with the end of funding (Davis, personal communication, 2010). How many countries have mechanisms to manage this kind of emerging research area in a systematic way? What mechanisms need to exist to identify areas in which research is needed and to link university researchers, with specialist expertise in neuroscience

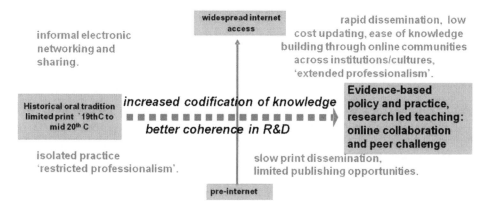

Figure 2. Increased codification of knowledge – moving from nineteenth-century to twenty-first-century professional practice.
Note: The contribution of Ralph Tabberer, chief executive of the Training and Development Agency for schools 2000–2007, to these ideas is acknowledged.
Source: Leask (2004a, 2004b).

and its implications for education, with system-wide groups of school-based teacher researchers? The development of such an international mechanism would facilitate the development of synergies rather than unnecessary replication. Networking university researchers in this area of education more effectively with teachers undertaking mini-research projects as part of their CPD could also provide some substantial research outcomes for both school and higher education sectors.

Reviews of current research in education[13] show that there is often considerable duplication across studies, and that much of the research undertaken is small scale. In addition, it may take many years for outcomes to be published and for others in the sector to hear about new research findings. Such replication could be avoided if the cycle of creating new knowledge, piloting new ideas and scaling up the research was supported by an international e-communications infrastructure, supporting communications between groups or individuals working on similar issues.[14]

In many countries, including Finland, Portugal and Norway, master's-level qualifications are now being expected of the teaching profession, and work undertaken at this level requires access to research. Without investment in the knowledge base for educational practice, however, and the means for accessing this, national funders of education systems are wasting considerable sums of money as professionals seek the knowledge needed for improvement through using the systems of yesteryear. Figure 2 illustrates these tensions.

Conclusions

This paper sets out various ways in which emerging technologies might be used to support effective CPD through knowledge management in the education sector. It also highlights opportunities taken up by the medical profession and by local government in the United Kingdom, but as yet ignored in the education sector. We have argued that effective CPD for educators requires effective knowledge management and outlined how an e-infrastructure at a national and an international level, allowing education professionals to find, manage, create and share new knowledge working with peers and experts (General Teaching Council for England 2006, Pickering *et al*. 2007), could support improvement in the quality of teacher knowledge. The argument is made that online services for knowledge-sharing and evidence-building for the education sector, which could support access to evidence to underpin practice and support both pre-service education and CPD, should be at least equivalent to those now available for the private sector and for the health and local government sectors (Davenport and Prusak 1998, Collison and Parcell 2006, Henley Knowledge Management Forum 2008a, 2008b, Wenger 1998, Wenger *et al*. 2002).

One test of whether or not sufficient and appropriate knowledge management tools exist for the education sector is if educators can keep up to date through accessing appropriate research-based knowledge to improve practice, at the time they need it and in the form they need it. A further test is whether educators are able to work collaboratively with peers and experts to co-construct new knowledge as changing circumstances require. For countries such as England where retention of teachers has historically been a problem (Education and Skills Committee 2004, p. 15), the costs of a system of ineffective CPD can be considerable in terms of human capital losses. There is then a clear logic to investment in an e-infrastructure, such as that proposed in this paper, to underpin a clear and effective CPD system. Any developments in this area in the future would, however, benefit from ensuring that sustainability is built in from the beginning since experience in England suggests that any provision online under state control may be lost when there is a change of government.

Acknowledgements

The authors gratefully acknowledge the following organisations that have funded the research which provided the evidence for this article: European Union, Training and Development Agency for Schools, and British Education Communications Technology Agency.

Notes

1. See http://www.eppi.ioe.ac.uk.
2. See http://www.tlrp.org/.
3. See http://nationalstrategies.standards.dcsf.gov.uk/.
4. See http://www.cochrane.org.
5. See http://www.cochrane.org.
6. See https://knowledgehub.local.gov.uk/.
7. IDeA was the improvement arm of the English Local Government Association. It was renamed Local Government Improvement and Development in 2011.
8. See https://knowledgehub.local.gov.uk/.
9. See http://www.eep.ac.uk and http://www.ttrb.ac.uk.
10. See http://www.teachernet.gov.uk and http://www.qcda.gov.uk.
11. See http://www.teachers.tv.
12. See http://www.mapofmedicine.com/.
13. See http://www.eppi.ioe.ac.uk.
14. An international network of leading schools, teacher training organisations and university teacher educators has now formed to take forward the ideas in this article. For further information, see http://www.edfuturescollaboration.org and http://www.educationcommunities.org.

References

Barber, M. and Mourshed, M., 2007. *How the world's best-performing school systems come out on top* [online]. London: McKinsey and Co. Available from: http://www.mckinsey.com/clientservice/Social_Sector/our_practices/Education/Knowledge_Highlights/Best_-performing_school.aspx [Accessed 18 June 2012].

Becta, 2008. *Harnessing technology review: the role of technology and its impact on education: full report* [online]. Coventry, UK: Becta, BEC1-15587. Available from: http://webarchive.nationalarchives.gov.uk/20101102103654/publications.becta.org.uk//display.cfm?resID=38751 [Accessed 18 June 2012].

Capel, S., Turner, T., and Leask, M., eds., 1994. *Learning to teach in the secondary school: a companion to school experience.* 1st ed. London: Routledge.

Capel, S., Turner, T., and Leask, M., eds., 2009. *Learning to teach in the secondary school: a companion to school experience.* 5th ed. London: Routledge.

Capel, S., Turner, T., and Leask, M., eds., 2013. *Learning to teach in the secondary school: a companion to school experience.* 6th ed. London: Routledge.

Carmichael, P. and Procter, R., 2006. *IT for education research: using new technology to enhance a complex research programme.* London: Institute of Education, Teaching and Learning Research Programme Research Briefing No. 16.

China Education and Research Network, 2000. *Teacher education in China (II). Remarkable results of reform and development of teacher education* [online]. Available from: http://www.edu.cn/20010101/21924.shtml [Accessed 18 June 2012].

Cochran-Smith, M. and Zeichner, K., 2005. *Studying teacher education: the report of the AERA panel on research and teacher education.* Washington, DC: American Educational Research Association in conjunction with Lawrence Erlbaum Associates, Mahwah, NJ.

Collison, C. and Parcell, G., 2006. *Learning to fly.* London: Wiley.

Davenport, T. and Prusak, L., 1998. *Working knowledge.* Boston, MA: Harvard Business School Press.

Davies, H., Nutley, S., and Smith, P., eds., 2000. *What works? Evidence-based policy and practice in public services.* Bristol: The Policy Press.

Department of Education, Employment and Workplace Relations, 2007. *Quality teachers, collaborative communities, effective learning.* Canberra: Commonwealth of Australia [online]. Available from: http://www.deewr.gov.au/Schooling/QualityTeaching/AGQTP/Documents/QualityTeachers.pdf [Accessed 18 June 2012].

Department of Education, Science and Training, 2005. *The emerging business of knowledge transfer: creating value from intellectual products and services* [online]. Canberra: Australian Government. Available from: http://www.dest.gov.au/NR/exeres/D11B0CCD-2BB0-437A-8260-0412E8921D4B.htm [Accessed 18 June 2012].

Education and Skills Committee, 2004. *Secondary education: teacher retention and recruitment.* Fifth Report of session 2003–2004, Volume 1. London: The Stationery Office, HC 1057–1 House of Commons.

General Teaching Council for England, 2006. *Synthesis of research and evaluation projects concerned with capacity-building through teachers' professional development: full research report* [online]. London: GTCE. Available from: http://www.gtce.org.uk/research/commissioned_research/cpd/synthesis_cpd_projects/ [Accessed 1 June 2011].

General Teaching Council for England, 2007. Making CPD better: Bringing together research about CPD: Leaflet [online]. Available from: http://www.gtce.org.uk/publications/res_cpd/ [Accessed 1 June 2011].

Grossman, P. and Thompson, C., 2008. Learning from curriculum materials: scaffolds for new teachers. *Teaching and teacher education,* 24 (8), 2014–2026.

Hammersley, M., 2002. *Educational research: policy-making and practice.* London: Paul Chapman.

Henley Knowledge Management Forum, 2008a. Building and sustaining communities of practice. *Knowledge in action.* Issue 07. Henley: Henley Management College.

Henley Knowledge Management Forum, 2008b. Sharing knowledge with other organisations. *Knowledge in action.* Issue 08. Henley: Henley Management College.

Improvement and Development Agency for Local Government, 2006. *Knowledge management strategy: board paper.* London: IDeA, IDeA internal document.

Improvement and Development Agency for Local Government, 2008. *Knowledge management tools and techniques: helping you find the right knowledge at the right time* [online]. London: IDeA. Available from: http://www.idea.gov.uk/idk/aio/8595069 [Accessed 18 June 2012].

Improvement and Development Agency for Local Government, 2009. *Communities of practice: internal research report.* London: IDeA.

Indian Government National Council for Teacher Education, 2010a. *Invitation for write-ups/contributions* [online]. Available from: http://www.ncte-india.org/publicnotice/invitation. pdf [Accessed 18 June 2012].

Indian Government National Council for Teacher Education, 2010b. *Awards to teacher educators in India* [online]. Available from: http://www.ncte-india.org/teacheraward.htm [Accessed 18 June 2012].

Kitchen, S., *et al.*, 2006. *Curriculum online evaluation: final report.* Coventry: Becta.

Laterza, V., Carmichael, P., and Procter, R., 2007. The doubtful guest? A virtual research environment for education. *Technology, pedagogy and education*, 16 (3), 249–267.

Lave, J. and Wenger, E., 1991. *Situated learning: legitimate peripheral participation.* Cambridge: Cambridge University Press.

Learning and Skills Network, 2008. *Measuring e-maturity in further education.* Coventry: Learning and Skills Network.

Leask, M., 2004a. Using research and evidence to improve teaching and learning in the training of professionals – an example from teacher training in England. *Paper presented at the British Educational Research Association Annual Conference*, 18 September, University of Manchester [online]. Available from: http://www.leeds.ac.uk/educol/documents/00003666.htm [Accessed 18 June 2012].

Leask, M., 2004b. Accumulating the evidence base for educational practice: our respective responsibilities. *Paper presented at the British Educational Research Association Annual Conference*, 18 September, University of Manchester [online]. Available from: http://www.leeds.ac.uk/educol/documents/00003665.htm [Accessed 18 June 2012].

Leask, M., 2012. Improving the professional knowledge base for education: using knowledge management and Web 2.0 tools. *Policy futures in education*, 9 (5), 644–660.

Leask, M. and Preston, C., 2010. *ICT tools for future teachers* [online]. Coventry: Becta. Available from: http://www.beds.ac.uk/__data/assets/pdf_file/0010/19459/ict-tools2009. pdf [Accessed 18 June 2012].

Leask, M. and Younie, S., 2001. Communal constructivist theory: pedagogy of information and communications technology and internationalisation of the curriculum. *Journal of information technology for teacher education*, 10 (1&2), 117–134.

Leask, M. and Younie. S., 2009a. *Submission to the Select Committee on Teacher Education.* Written evidence submitted on behalf of the IT in Teacher Education professional association and Brunel University [online]. London: House of Commons Children, Schools and Families Select Committee. Available from: http://www.publications.parliament.uk/pa/cm200809/cmselect/cmchilsch/memo/teactrai/tetr3702.htm [Accessed 18 June 2012].

Leask, M. and Younie, S., 2009b. *Use of learning platforms to support continuing professional development in HEIs and schools.* Coventry: Becta.

Loughran, J., 2006. *Developing a pedagogy of teacher education: understanding teaching and learning about teaching.* Abingdon: Routledge.

Ming-yuan, G., 2006. The reform and development in teacher education in China. *Beijing Normal University Keynote speech in the First International Forum on Teacher Education*, 25–27 October, Shanghai, China [online]. Available from: http://www.icte.ecnu. edu.cn/EN/show.asp?id=547 [Accessed 18 June 2012].

Newman, M., Elbourne, D., and Leask, M., 2004. Improving the usability of educational research: guidelines for the reporting of empirical primary research studies in education. *Roundtable discussion paper presented at the 5th Annual Conference of the Teaching and Learning Research Programme*, 22–24 November, Cardiff.

Oakley, A., 2003. Research evidence, knowledge management and educational practice: early lessons from a systematic approach. *London review of education*, 1 (1), 21–34.

OECD, 2007a. *Understanding the brain: the birth of a learning science.* Paris: OECD/CERI.

OECD, 2007b. *Evidence in education: linking research and policy.* Paris: OECD.

OECD, 2009a. *Creating effective teaching and learning environments: first results from teaching and learning international survey (TALIS)* [online]. Available from: http://www.oecd.org/document/54/0,3343,en_2649_39263231_42980662_1_1_1_1,00.html [Accessed 18 June 2012].

OECD, 2009b. *Education at a glance 2009: OECD indicators* [online]. Available from: http://www.oecd.org/document/24/0,3343,en_2649_39263238_43586328_1_1_1_1,00.html [Accessed 18 June 2012].

OECD, 2010. *Education lighthouse* [online]. Paris: Organisation for Economic Cooperation and Development. Available from: http://www.oecd.org/document/61/0,3343, en_2649_33723_42992189_1_1_1_1,00.html [Accessed 18 June 2012].

Pickering, J., Daly, C., and Pachler, N., eds., 2007. *New designs for teachers' professional learning*. London: Bedford Way Papers. Institute of Education, University of London.

Procter, R., 2007. Collaboration, coherence and capacity-building: the role of DSpace in supporting and understanding the TLRP. *Technology, pedagogy and education*, 16 (3), 269–288.

Shulman, L., 1987. Knowledge and teaching: foundation of a new reform. *Harvard educational review*, 57 (1), 1–22.

Smith, P., Rudd, P., and Coghlan, M., 2008. *Harnessing technology: schools survey 2008 report 1: analysis*. Coventry: Becta.

Taylor, C., *et al.*, 2008. *Evaluation of the Applied Educational Research Scheme* [online]. Edinburgh: Education Information and Analytical Services, Scottish Government. Available from: http://www.scotland.gov.uk/Publications/2008/01/07140223/0 [Accessed 19 June 2012].

UNESCO, 2010a. *Qualifying and training teachers in Brazil*. Paris: UNESCO.

UNESCO, 2010b. *The Teacher Training Initiative for sub-Saharan Africa (TTISSA)* [online]. Paris: UNESCO. Available from: http://www.unesco.org/en/teacher-education/ [Accessed 18 June 2012].

Wenger, E., 1998. *Communities of practice: learning, meaning, and identity*. Cambridge, MA: Cambridge University Press.

Wenger, E., McDermott, R., and Snyder, W., 2002. *Cultivating communities of practice: a guide to managing knowledge*. Cambridge, MA: Harvard Business School Press.

Index